Breaking Through is a courageous and tender book that takes the heart to the hell of abuse and the hope of redemption. It is a walk through the valley of death, but in many ways it is not the pain that will be remembered, but the fragrance of God's paradoxical work of drawing forth life from death and hope from despair.

Cathy Ann allows us to walk with her to comprehend what it means to face life head on, grieve our losses and grow in the wonder of God's forgiveness. Whether your life has a history of abuse or not, this is a lesson in living that will win your heart that much more for good.

Dan Allender, Ph.D.
Colorado Christian University, USA.
Author, *The Wounded Heart.*

This book gave me a shot at life. I held it, read it over and over, underlined it, even memorized parts. It told me I was not alone, someone had actually survived the devastating consequences of child sexual abuse and was getting on with her life. The hope, courage and determination this gave me were irreplaceable. I saw God had got Cathy Ann where she was and that hanging on to Him was the only way out. Although my church let me down, I hung on to Christ's cross, my trusted bible in my hand and *Breaking Through* tucked under arm.

Miss Jamie Torrens.
Survivor.

Breaking Through has been a great help to thousands of people for thousands of reasons. People who have suffered sexual abuse are encouraged by this book to pursue the journey to recovery. It helps survivors in their struggle to believe that God is good and caring and enables others to gain deeper empathy and greater wisdom.

Rev. Michael Corbett-Jones.
Director, Anglican Counselling Centre, Sydney, Australia.
Registered psychologist.

Cathy Ann Matthews has been a pioneer in helping Christians to deal with the trauma of child sexual abuse. Her life and her work have been an inspiration to countless people in Australia and beyond. This book, of both great sadness and joy, illuminates a path for others to follow. It shows how much some children suffer yet how God can help heal even the deepest hurts.

Patrick Parkinson.
Associate Professor of Law, Sydney University, Australia.
Author, *Child Sexual Abuse and the Church.*

With a quiet dignity, Cathy Ann Matthews has journeyed beyond her own personal pain to bring a message of hope to fellow sufferers. This books excels in the use of plain English to express profound depths of emotion and reflects the author's sensitive respect for the spiritual dimension of personality.

Dr. Elizabeth MacMahon, GP.
National Medical Advisor,
National Association for the Prevention of Child Abuse and Neglect, Australia.

While there are now many books covering the subject of child abuse, this one includes many elements that make it uniquely valuable for survivors and supporters alike. Not a textbook, but a manual: not prescriptive in a dogmatic way, but descriptive of what can help; not a commentary, but the account of a personal journey which, in company with others, leads beyond the pain and shame to emerge into the sunlight. Truly a hopeful book.

John Court, Ph.D.
Former Prolessor of Psychology,
Fuller Theological Seminary, Pasadena, USA.

BREAKING THROUGH

Cathy Ann Matthews

BREAKING THROUGH

No longer a victim of child abuse

Contents

Foreword   7
Introduction   9
Acknowledgements   13

PART ONE: JOURNEY THROUGH PAIN
1   The locked past   19
2   The poison pen   24
3   The revealing catscan   31
4   The spider hunt   40
5   The family dinner   48
6   The two daddies   57
7   The heartbreaking secret   62
8   The cushion room   71
9   The unutterable loneliness   80
10   The parental bonds   89

PART TWO: *ROAD MAP FOR SURVIVORS*

11   Our common hopeful place   *103*

12   Our common hurting place   *113*

PART THREE: *STEPS TO RECOVERY*

13   My first step: *Listen to me!*   *127*

14   My second step: *This is me!*   *139*

15   My third step: *Manage me!*   *153*

16   My fourth step: *Amplify it for me!*   *168*

17   My fifth step: *Speak to me!*   *179*

18   My sixth step: *I grieve for me!*   *193*

19   My seventh step: *Release me!*   *208*

20   My eighth step: *I choose to forgive!*   *220*

Foreword

IT IS ONLY RELATIVELY RECENTLY that we have learnt about the extent and seriousness of child abuse. First, it was from descriptions of physical abuse: from children who were seriously injured by those who were supposed to nurture and protect them their parents. Then sexual abuse became a subject which could be talked about openly and, with that, came the discovery that the sexual abuse of children, boys as well as girls, is perhaps as common as physical abuse.

We are now starting to learn about emotional abuse: the belittling and degrading of children by those who are supposed to nurture them and build up their self-esteem. Emotional abuse is something which is present in all forms of abuse because of the message that the child receives from the adult: that the child is the adult's property and worthless – except to be used to gratify the adult's own needs.

What we are also discovering is that it is not just the abusive episodes which are harmful to the child: it is also what the abuse does to the child's developing self. How can a child learn to trust, to feel worthwhile, to give and accept love if that child's model – the parent, or another trusted adult who should have been relied upon to encourage and value the child – made the child feel worthless? What if their love was not unconditional?

For many abused children the hurt continues well into

their adult lives. They feel, because they were not valued by their parents, that they are of no value. They feel that the abuse was their fault because they were not good enough to earn their parents' love.

Cathy Ann Matthews, the author of this book, was an abused child. She was abused physically, sexually and emotionally. This book is her story about how she came to understand the darker side of her childhood and how she struggled to find emotional well-being and peace. She talks about her anger and her frustrations as she struggled to understand why this had to happen to her. There is refreshing candour here as she frankly describes feelings and doubts which many people will relate to, but to which perhaps few would readily admit. Cathy Ann Matthews' honesty, humour and the steps she describes to obtain inner healing have something to say to all adults who were abused as children and to those who have to learn to understand the pain which many still carry.

There is much to learn from the experiences revealed in *Breaking Through*.

Kim Oates
Professor of Paediatrics & Child Health
The University of Sydney
President, International Society for the
Prevention of Child Abuse and Neglect
February, 1990

Introduction

MY HISTORY WILL ALWAYS READ. . . *abused as a child!* Now there is hope. The control of abuse is broken, yet its repressed memories, hidden from my conscious mind for forty years, had set up consequences of pain, self-hatred and fear.

Everyone hurts, everyone has endured some mistreatment as a child. Even those who had the most favoured childhood have been misunderstood and misdirected, or have known failure in care and attention, no matter how slight. No-one escapes pain and trouble in this life. But for thousands of children there is a stage when a child becomes the passive, helpless victim of the maltreatment of another person: *that child is being abused!*

The situation for each of these children has moved into another dimension, that of cruelty, lust or deprivation. This ill-treatment may – in fact very likely will – have painful consequences which can continue into their adult lives. It is especially for such hurting adults and their supporters that I have written this book. I want them to know there is hope of an ongoing recovery.

When the memories of my abuse began to return I needed to tell my story and I wanted others who had been abused to know that I have been there too; they are not alone in their heartache and pain. My first book, *No Longer a Victim,* the story of my childhood, became part of my therapy as it poured on to paper in much anguish.

How could I face the horrors that were erupting into my present life, spilling their agony over my externally ordered existence? How could I deal with the devastating internal repercussions which had plagued me through my life? How could I cope? I knew I needed a method which helped me twenty-four hours of each day to come to grips with the returning memories and the adaptions I had made to that terrible childhood. Gradually over that time of reliving I began using a set of steps, which were implicit through *No Longer a Victim*, though not clearly defined. When I was asked to speak about my continuing recovery to other survivors and those who counsel and support us, I began to formulate these steps more clearly.

I appreciated the suggestion to combine *No Longer a Victim* with the steps to recovery. So this present book, *Breaking Through*, begins with the abuse in my childhood and my journey through that pain. It is followed by an explanation of many of the adverse effects of abuse and shows us how to move from despair to hope. This section of the book acts as the connecting link with the practical steps I took to enable me to be released from my childhood.

In breaking through, not only was I facing my childhood, but also another problem which caused me deep misery and had to be dealt with. It was my struggle to come to terms with the dichotomy between my belief that God cared for and loved me, and my feelings of rejection by him. Many survivors have told me how they, too, have felt rejected by God and feel they cannot trust him. I know how hard it is for victims of child abuse to trust God. I understand the reactions of anger and hatred against him felt by many survivors and their families and others who support them. Facing these problems in myself has played a large part in my recovery.

I know also that some who read this book might be opposed to, or just not be interested in religion, but I cannot tell my story unless I share with you God's participation in my recovery. For despite my damaged faith I believe God worked constructively in my life. Under his direction I have embarked on a lifetime project of using the steps. These are bringing about a change in me; I am being released from my past with its dominating control from my abusing parents. I am breaking through, like sun after rain, into a new way of viewing myself, at last beginning to see and acknowledge those worthwhile attributes which are mine, and I'm learning to know God better. All this is leading me to wholeness and freedom and growth.

I don't have answers to all my questions. Nor do I have all the answers for those who have been abused. What I have I've gladly given. I'm offering you the path I took through my suffering; a way which won't let you ignore your pain or escape from it. This path won't be easy and it will require from you much hard, painful and time-consuming work. Even so, I hope you will find encouragement from the steps I took to lead you through the horrors of your abuse into a better, more satisfying existence.

Nothing can change the fact that we survivors were abused. Nevertheless, I'm convinced that we do not have to stay bound by its effects; we can make a choice. What we do with the emotional scars from our abuse can disfigure or adorn our tomorrows.

Acknowledgements

WRITING THIS BOOK was quite a struggle, so I'm particularly grateful to all those people who have encouraged me, not only as I wrote, but also as I faced my childhood traumas. There were days, enlightened and dark, when I knew you were praying and I sank back into the net of your prayers to think, rest and be renewed; my sincere thanks for your love, support and prayers. As well, I am grateful to God for hearing and answering our prayers. Some of my supporters deserve an extra mention. . .

Firstly to my husband, whose patience in listening, rereading, querying, suggesting and in general being there for me to bounce my thoughts off and cry with – my warmest thanks. Thankyou especially for staying steady at those times when the whole experience stretched our relationship in all directions. To my children I want to say thankyou for your love and understanding, because I know you were hurting, too. To my sister, thanks for remembering with me and for your great sense of humour; all the laughs really helped.

The special editing expertise which Ken Goodlet, Mamie Long and Ruth Drobnak put at my disposal, toiling for long hours over a hot manuscript, was gladly accepted, much appreciated and very helpful. My thanks go to my talented and unselfish friends, Alison Reid and Shona Kinnear, who gave me willingly of their counselling skills and their grasp of the problems of adult survivors; and to John Mallison, who inspired me with creative suggestions.

I am also grateful to those who brought the documentary drama film of the book to fruition. My special thanks to Richard Mason who had the courage, tenacity and ability to produce such a topic on film; to Steve Mason for his vision, commitment and camera artistry; to Jackie McKimmie for warm, sensitive directing; to the cast for their understanding and faithful portrayal of the nuances of my writing; and to a great crew for unselfish dedication.

Thankyou all for your contribution to my *Breaking Through*!

PART ONE:

JOURNEY THROUGH PAIN

No longer a victim!

To wander through the far reaches of my mind
is to enter again that first place for me.
My initial memories. I know them well.
Such expectations! Others demur, their belief uncertain.
>   Lightly I laugh, for from the first
>   I was aware of my potential
>   for joy, enthusiasm, love.

The unshakable knowledge that life held for me
an open door to fulfilment
assured acceptance of my own possibilities,
thwarted by years of callous debasement.
>   Those years of childhood, of sham and shame,
>   loved yet beaten, hated yet caressed,
>   used, misused, abused.

The teen years, awkwardly coping with the confusion
of their troughs and peaks. Straining to become adult,
whilst clinging in desperation to a childhood
imagined to be as it never was.
>   For I repressed it, unknowingly,
>   behind a believed facade. The victim
>   of lies, cruelty, fear.

Struggling always to bring forth my God-given gifts,
longing for my parents to hold me of value.
But they, tossed between relief and guilt,
shattered me by the force of their non-acceptance.
    A brutal rejection.
    I – an unwanted intruder, their failed abortion.
    But I'll take courage, hope, faith.

I'll not stay strangled by their wrong assessment,
hopes made counterfeit. . . never to know completion.
I'll bear the unbearable, emerge scarred but victorious.
The chain of abuse broken by love.
    Set free by God's Spirit, I'll face the future
    no longer a victim!
    Valued, loved and accepted.

1
The locked past

REPRESSION HAS BURST ITS BONDS and in its telling I find release, as also in the tears. Tears I could not weep when I was a little girl: tears of fear, rejection and pain so deep the memory has lain hidden, smouldering for forty years. It vanished within me. . . forced out of my conscious remembrance by the very weight of its horror, too terrible for me to cope with, too heartbreaking for me to live with.

Now, as though doors have been flung open, those first fifteen years of my life are bursting forth with an agony almost beyond endurance and I am forced to share.

Yet I am afraid of writing. I shrink from committing pen to paper, still another of those previously inexplicable fears which seem to have haunted my life. But now as I see it here staring back at me, made all splodgy with my tears, I can no longer deny the evidence. Here is the truth of my childhood, my hidden existence: *I was an abused child. Unwanted. . . battered. . . unloved!*

These repugnant discoveries which keep erupting out of my subconscious cannot be the truth – just some weird distortion of my mind!

How I long to cast them from me and shout for all to hear: 'Not true. . . Not true. My parents did love me, they did not hurt me!'

But no, it really did happen. It is true, as my sister Clare so gently confirmed. 'At last you, too, are opening your Pandora's box,' she said.

How tightly it was locked. I could not have guessed at its contents or of its existence, except for the deep unhappiness, unrelated to my present life, which lay just below the surface of my mind, thinly veiled from the view of others.

Now I was in my fifties trying to live as normal a life as possible, appearing to the outside world as a smiling, friendly, rather proper religious person, apparently coping and with no obvious reason for not doing so, yet not knowing why I felt such internal anguish. However, much as I desired it, I knew I was not at peace with God. As religion is so much part of my story, I must include my struggles to find peace and to come to grips with the conflict between my belief in a loving God and the horror of my childhood abuse.

As these traumas from my childhood are being disclosed to my conscious mind, consolidating into sad reality, an understandable cause for my feelings is presenting itself: the cruelty of my parents. Many of my former debilitating fears are gradually being explained. So much that has been a way of coping – a behavioural pattern, set up to enable me to keep facing life, to stop my mind from shattering – is now just beginning to be understood.

The events of my childhood have somehow produced a wall, dividing my memory into two nearly distinct, unconnected lives. In some experiences the two become entwined; they mesh together, forming a fully remembered picture. Others, as yet unable to be integrated, stay as isolated incidents, perhaps never to form into the pattern of one whole life.

I do not know when, or where, another piece of the jigsaw of my life will flip from the unknown to the known. It could be evoked by a word, a smell, a look or an action, such as lying in bed, stretching out my hand for a jar of face cream, and suddenly being startled to hear the stifled sobbing of my own childish voice, as I lay hiding under the bedclothes

trying to keep the sound muffled for fear of a worse punishment than had already been administered. It could be the
lovely music of Tchaikovsky, reminding me of a radio serial
we listened to as kids, bringing back to me a part of my
personality which had seemed lost for ever.

It was just eight years ago that these discoveries began to
be revealed to me. Until then, I had only remembered a
fairly normal childhood: externally happy, an ordinary,
everyday suburban home, with what seemed to my memory
a few idiosyncrasies, unique to our family.

I was a bright, moderately intelligent child, given to
sickness and not very robust. Fairly turbulent teen years
followed, which my outgoing personality was able to fill with
many friends and fun, though still dogged with illnesses.

In my twenties I met Robert, a special man, and fell in
love with him and his delightful humour. Learning together
of God and dedicating our lives to him, we entered happily
into marriage. For both of us it was a time full of love and
sharing, with Rob becoming a clergyman.

The next thirty years together were full of interest and
diversity: changing homes frequently, moving interstate,
travelling overseas, missionary work and three vital children.
Sarah, Grace and Bartholomew have been a constant source
of love, frustration and joy for us. They have led unusual
lives, each displaying their individuality in ways not always
of our choosing. Generally we respect and delight in their
uniqueness, praying that they will learn to relate to God in a
way which meets their own needs, not swayed by the confusion and turmoil which has often shaken my faith. Each
one of my family has been affected, I know, in their own way
by my inner fears and pain and by my doubts about God.

Quite a fulfilling life, yet through it all, something inside
me stalked my very existence. Such fear and torment lay
behind my smiling, oh-so-polite facade. What caused the
anguish, the utterly debilitating and incapacitating exhaustion, the enveloping cloak of depression which haunted my

days and kept me awake relentlessly searching for sleep into the small hours night after night? Why the self-hatred, the self-denigration, the sense of complete worthlessness? Why the longing for death as a release from the frenetic activity of my thoughts? Why the always imminent fear of my mind tipping over some unknown precipice into a vast chasm of insanity? Just occasionally it all lay dormant; at other times it screamed within me, throwing me into a despair which disrupted our lives and undermined my physical and emotional health.

Rob was helpful and considerate, trying to comprehend my anxiety and coping when I had several trips to hospital in an endeavour to discover the cause of my problem.

Private hopelessness saturated my being, for its cause was completely unknown.

One day, in the throes of deep despair, too depressed even to get out of bed, I poured out my heartache to God, begging him to do something to help us before the burden became more than I could bear and I was driven to take my life. These were not mere words, but a prayer wrung from me with an intensity that wrenched me out of my bed and on to my knees.

In the depths of my need, God began a painful yet extraordinary work towards my healing. He answered lovingly, patiently, yet with set purpose, moving me inexorably on. Soon after, I remember boarding a bus which jerked forward, swerving out into the traffic. Bumping my way down the aisle, I chose a seat, scrambled in and, entirely oblivious of my surroundings, an impelling new idea slid into my mind: What if God is not as I have always thought? Amazed, I tried to grapple with this revelation. What if my innermost convictions of God are entirely wrong?

'My innermost convictions': here was where the confusion lay, not in my conscious mind with its beliefs in a good, trustworthy and loving God. These facts I held on to, had taken for my own over thirty years before. But, underneath, in my feelings and emotions, another comprehending of God had been working in its subtle way.

My emotions insisted: 'God cannot be believed. . . God cannot be trusted. . . he does not love me.'

The bus rattled on. . .

A stillness gradually diffused into every part of my being, the quieting of an awful inner turmoil. This sense of peace, uncommon for me, gently pervaded my person until, at last, I was able to think more calmly: 'Perhaps God does love me . . . perhaps he can be trusted.'

It wasn't until later that the inevitable queries arose. What stood between my intellectual beliefs in God and my fear and distrust of him? What was the wall which divided my external coping existence from my hurting inner self?

2

The poison pen

WALLS MAKE GREAT BARRIERS; they keep intruders out and prisoners in. Walls have doors; doors can be opened, must be opened, to let friends in and the homeowner out into the world. When doors open, light floods into the room behind the wall.

I had a wall. No-one knew of its existence, nor what lay behind it. My wall had a door also, and I was banging on it, trying desperately to force it open to release whatever was pushing against it, while at the same time consuming vast amounts of energy keeping my past in its repressed state and pretending all was well.

Now it seemed God's time had come. He began to unlock that door. He did it as he considered right, although for me it was some years before I was able to see and even accept how carefully he had prepared me for this moment. He opened it slowly when I started training to become a marriage counsellor, an experience that taught me some of the fundamentals of how my mind operates.

Looking back, it did not seem surprising to Rob and me that our decision to train as marriage counsellors and help others was the very key which opened the door and so helped me. For here was God's opportunity to enable me to look at and face my past, in as safe and controlled a situation as possible. Now that the girls were adults and had moved out, and Bart our son was seeking his independence, my duties and privileges of family-raising were past. 'It's your time now,' my eldest daughter Sarah said.

It was indeed time to work on my life.

Part of my training was to sit in with a qualified counsellor several times a week and attend lectures and interaction with a group. I found it so worthwhile sitting in with the counsellor, Tessa, as she listened and accepted the client's feelings. Could it be possible that I, too, could share some of my inner haunted person with this caring lady? Gradually we began to share the more superficial aspects of my life, where I brought to mind things from my childhood: my mother's laughter, which for some obscure reason seemed to trouble me.

'What about your father?' queried my counsellor later.

'Oh! We had a great relationship. . . went through a patch of hating during my teens, but I grew out of that and we were very close and loving again, as always. He was so handsome, so tall, so strong. There's just one thing I do remember, though. He used to play chasings with us around the garden. I was so afraid of being caught. The price of capture was to be tickled. . . mercilessly. . . he would stand on my feet so I couldn't get away. I always wanted to vomit; it wasn't very nice.'

'You didn't like being tickled and feeling sick?' Tessa asked.

'No – it was awful!'

Again the counsellor queried: 'Is Daddy hurting you?'

To which I mumbled a puzzled 'Yes'.

Counsellor: 'Tell Daddy – "You're hurting me, Daddy".'

'Oh Daddy! You're hurting me!'

Tears welled up in my eyes and flowed down my face. My head sank on to my arm and I wept.

What information was this? My father had hurt me. What could it mean? I knew without doubt that it had been a deliberate action on his part.

The next time I returned for counselling an awareness had arisen in me of a fear of my father. Oh well, best to find out what it was all about. My counsellor gently stayed with this feeling of fear. I remembered Dad used to beat me, but something else stirred within me. I became aware of him sitting at our dining table, writing letters. He would read them to us: vindictive, abusive letters. I could see his fountain pen.

'No! No! Not that pen! That awful pen!' Within a minute I was back there. . . a little girl. . . three to four years old.

Terrible sounds of pain and anguish began to arise from within me: shocking, shattering sounds, breaking forth from some deep, deep place as though something imprisoned innumerable years ago was surfacing with frightening intensity.

I staggered up from my chair, unable to remain seated, as my very being tore itself loose from its habitual moorings.

'Must hide. . . Here's a corner. . . Hide! Hide! Nowhere to hide.' I blundered around that little office, my counsellor snatching chairs away as I reeled towards them, falling against the wall, feeling its coldness on my face. . . and yet I was a little girl, filled with an inexplicable terror.

Tessa's voice: 'Your Daddy beat you?'

Oh! If only that was all I was discovering and reliving: a beating. I knew I'd had those. It wasn't the beatings that were producing that stabbing, terrifying, pain-filled response. It was. . . this fountain pen! Somehow seeing it again caused these repressed memories to burst forth:

> He is drawing on me with it. Rude, crude drawings, all on my body. What do they mean? I don't understand. Oh no! He's drawing targets. . . dart boards. . . on me!
> I hear his voice, strangely menacing: 'Now child, stand over there!'
> I mustn't cry out. . . must stand very still. I'm so afraid. He's aiming that fountain pen at. . . *me*!
> 'You can't be going to do that, Daddy!'

There's just a little rushing breeze as that pen passes by my body. He missed. . . it was always the same.

He always missed, or didn't even throw. I think it was the fear he wanted to engender which seemed to give him the stimulus he craved. Finally the crying ceased. . . the little girl faded. I was spent.

Where was the truth in all of this? How could I believe what had just happened? Had I invented all this horror? I knew I had never read such gruesome things as were now being revealed to me. Could they be true? Shock, confusion and exhaustion overwhelmed me. My beloved husband came and took me home.

Later the words of Jesus came crashing into my mind: 'You shall know the truth and the truth shall set you free.' I had always thought that statement spoke about the truths of God's love and forgiveness, though sadly I wasn't always too certain of these. But maybe it meant all truth, even this truth about myself which I needed to know, and which I was absolutely terrified to discover.

In my conscious mind I could remember none of it. I had to know if it was true. Where could I find out? Who to ask? My parents were dead and I could never have asked them anyway. That left my sister Clare: I must contact her. She and I were never very close. A barrier not easily understood was always there between us. We wanted to be loving and sisterly, but seemed unable to break through to each other and now I had to ask her about these terrible things which were erupting from my past. I rang her, suggesting she come and visit. She realised something unusual was happening to me and came.

How was I to broach this most delicate subject? After several attempts, and spilling a cup of coffee over her in my agitation, she came to my rescue. Sitting me down quietly, she said, 'Ann, our father was a handler!'

Oh! The relief. . . she knew! It wasn't just in my mind,

my imagination. . . she *knew!*

I began to pour out my discovery, while she nodded and agreed. 'Yes, that's right – I remember.' She had remembered it all and could never understand why in the past I would not discuss it. Poor Clare! She'd had to live with it all alone for so long. Now we could share, carefully, for she was far from well, recovering from heart bypass surgery. Since then, not once has she related an incident, but rather has let me tell her what has come back to my memory, and then, as she gently makes me share the minute details – the age I was, where it took place, colours and times – she has verified my discoveries.

We discussed our parents. Mother was small yet vital, always seeking the limelight, noisy and gregarious. She was an A grade tennis player until heart trouble made her an invalid when I was seventeen. She died at fifty-five, just before I turned twenty-eight and had my first child. My father lived another sixteen years and died suddenly when he was seventy-one years of age. He lived part of that time with us and my children remember him well. They were deeply hurt and shocked by my later discoveries.

Father had been a bookkeeper in the city until his retirement. He was a large man, domineering and always right. He spent his spare time in the garden growing fruit and vegetables and beautiful flowers ('Yuk! Pink dahlias,' muttered Clare). These he proudly shared with his fellow workers.

Who could have guessed at the horrors he perpetrated upon us in that garden and in that neat brick house, in that ordinary street, in that middle-class suburb? For my parents appeared to everyone as upright, honest, respectable citizens, and I always believed I loved them.

Yet, now that I have discovered these other truths about them, I realise that as a little child I was unable to take in the enormity of it all and so it was repressed. I could not cope with the deception – the absolute dichotomy between the facts and the facade – of their displaying to the world the image of a happy, loving family.

Timmy our cat

*My daddy is sad
'cause Timmy our cat
was attacked by dogs,
left hurt and broken.*

*My daddy is angry.
'I'll get those b----- owners
for not protecting
this helpless creature.'*

*My daddy is comforting.
He said, 'How are you,
poor fellow?
I'll stroke you better.'*

*My daddy beat us.
'Why must we pay
for Daddy's fury
at others' cruelty?'*

My daddy loves Tim.
He must be of value;
his wounds are treated
and tenderly cared for.

'My daddy, see me
all hurt and broken?
Do I have some value –
as much as a cat?'

'My daddy, I'm here,
confused and feeling
the awful pain
of that needless attack.'

My daddy is crying
'cause our cat is dying,
while I'm just wishing
I was Timmy our cat!

3

The revealing catscan

THE DISPLAY had become the reality for me.

How amazing the mind is! Mine had completely blotted out all the memories associated with my parents' cruelty and had built a whole childhood and teen years upon the episodes which appeared normal and mainly pleasant. Consciously I can only bring back parts of my life. I can only move along one side of my partitioning wall. I am still clinging desperately to such acceptable memories as the happy family and the parents who loved me. I do not want to see that other picture, the one locked away, the one that gnaws at my internal being and tortures my consciousness with an indefinable agony.

So I will look at the life I do remember. I will recall the picture of my childhood as I have consciously held it in my mind all these years and believed it to be. I will try to think about my parents clearly, try to recall the facts I know about them.

I loved them. They seemed normal parents to me and, looking back, I saw an apparently contented, though shy little girl with a mummy and daddy who fed me and dressed me, sent me to school, had me taught the piano and did all the usual things caring parents do. They seem, now, to have been excessively strict and hard on us. But even though that was difficult, it was compensated for, because my daddy often sat me on his knee and cuddled me and my mummy looked after me when I was sick (though she did leave me at home by myself often, but of course she had to play her tennis matches).

What did I know about the background of these two people, my parents? Mainly what they had told me. My mother had come from a prosperous, well-to-do business family of six children. She often told me that the girls in her family had not been treated as well as the boys and she considered this an injustice which seemed to have coloured her life. She was friendly with one brother and sister and their children. Both her parents were dead and Clare and I never had the special pleasure and nurture that grandparents can sometimes give.

My father was the third of five brothers and sisters. He had practically cut himself off from his family in the country and was fairly self-sufficient by his mid-teens. Being very tall, he was able to join the army at the age of seventeen and was posted overseas during World War I. He spoke disparagingly of his army time and blamed it for affecting his life.

He married my mother about eight years after the war and Clare was born within two years – a difficult birth, Mum always said – and I was born eighteen months later. Father renewed his contact with his brothers and sisters then, so we saw them and our cousins occasionally. But usually we kept to ourselves as a family and I remember Clare and I happily playing and laughing together when we were very young. I always thought Clare was beautiful with her wonderful golden curls, and I never understood why she became so serious. I was expected to be the sunny one.

Sometimes we used to go for picnics to the beach, but we always had to be so proper in public that they weren't much fun. When we stopped going after I turned eight, I didn't mind too much and was content to just play at home in our garden. We weren't ever allowed to go to other children's homes to play; Mummy used to say it wasn't safe!

Daddy built me a cubby-house once, but it was dark and gloomy inside and he kept coming in and making me all squashed and crowded, so I wouldn't play in it any more.

After dinner some nights, until I was about six, we had fun together. Mummy would sing all the old songs, and Clare and I were allowed to comb Daddy's hair and put bows in its thick dark waves. I caught the comb in it once and it had to be cut out with a chunk of hair. Daddy was furious, because he always had to look 'just right', so that was the last time we ever did that.

It seems odd now, thinking back over it, how often as we grew older we carried Mum to bed after she had fallen fast asleep at the dinner table. Now I ask myself, startled by the thought, why would this perfectly healthy, sporty lady fall asleep after the evening meal and have to be carried to bed? In time I was to find the answer. Secretly I thought she didn't like washing up. I didn't. Dad used to laugh and make curious jokes about it, but beneath the pleasantries I still remember the undercurrent of fear and the absolute terror in case I dropped Mummy's leg as we struggled to carry her through the hall and into her bedroom.

Every year till I was twelve we went for a holiday to a lake and spent our time swimming, fishing and playing – outwardly happy. Sometimes Daddy gave us an interesting package to take on the train. We would watch with growing excitement for a chosen railway station, because then we could open our parcel and eat its exciting contents, always lollies, a special treat during those years of the Great Depression. I loved it when Daddy did things like that and I clung onto those memories as though they were the only reality.

Strangely though, before each of these holidays, I would go secretly through our garden and meticulously move from one plant and tree to the next, bidding them farewell, overwhelmed by the thought that I was never going to return, as though each holiday held for me a nameless fear. I would kiss our old cat Timmy goodbye and whistle a while with the canary, infinitely sad within myself because I was going away. Yet it was only for a holiday!

Now I realise it meant that day after day I had to be careful and on guard because I did not know what Daddy was planning to do next: like the way he would hold our heads under water till we could hardly breathe. He said it was to help us with our swimming. During those holidays, for twenty-four hours every day, I would never be free of his presence and never feel safe. Until my new discoveries, that whole farewell process had always seemed peculiar to me.

So much of my childhood was bound up with Clare: how did she fit into these pictures?

Clare, having remembered it all, had at an early age withdrawn from intimate contact with family or friends and retreated into books. She spent her time reading, constantly reading, now and then endeavouring to stand up to Father, which I thought was tremendously brave of her, but being sneered at and broken with vicious words and by the sheer dominance of his will and his overbearing adulthood. Added to this for Clare was the discovery of a neglected birth defect, diagnosed when she was about nine, which meant that from then on she went regularly to a hospital for treatment. It caused her untold suffering: its only good effect was that it restrained my father from physically abusing her again.

Clare and I wanted to be friends and share together, but both our parents widened the gap between us by subtly undermining and playing off one against the other with nasty remarks and lies aimed at belittling. Often at night, after we went to bed, we would begin to whisper together, then Father's heavy tread would be heard steadily approaching down the hall and his huge bulk would fill our doorway and in that low-pitched yet menacing voice he would forbid us to speak to each other.

'If I catch you talking to each other I'll punish you,' he'd say. That was enough to stop us from much sharing at all, so we only bickered as children will and kept our distance from each other. The consequences were too devastating and the lying innuendoes too strong for our affection for each other to overcome.

Another unusual thing I remember was that during World War II our clothes seemed to become rather ragged and there was never quite enough to eat. An old school friend I met recently told me, 'You sure were a skinny kid. . .' Father was taking our food coupons into his office as he said his friends needed them. He told us we must all do our bit, so this was our contribution to Father's war effort and our boost to his secretly insatiable desire for self-aggrandisement. To me, it seemed a strange way to help. We became thin and sickly.

Did they really look after us properly? Even now I haven't come to grips fully with that question. There are gaps in my memories of my parents which nothing or no-one seems able to fill.

Thinking back, Mum's housekeeping and cooking were decidedly uninspired, but she could be such pleasant company and I liked her. She had not been well for some time. Over the last few years before she died, she was an invalid. I nursed her and thought her courageous to endure the pain of her heart attacks and still be able to laugh and make jokes. She had long ago given up her beloved tennis, golf and dancing which had filled most of her time when we were young. And by now she could no longer go to the card parties and bingo nights which had become her life, though I knew she had many cultural interests and was an entertaining conversationalist.

Over that time we enjoyed each other's company, but looking back to when we were younger I seemed to remember her as rather loudmouthed and bawdy, for during my teen years she told off-colour jokes to any young man who came to our house. Clare and I never got those jokes; we remained surprisingly innocent for all our mistreatment. A while before Mother died, she found a faith in God and often asked me was she really forgiven by him, but never once did she mention the reasons for this frequent question.

I wonder whether she was ill-treated by my father? Had she married this handsome young man to discover he was sadistic and cruel? If so, how had she coped? What had their sexual relationship been like? In those days that subject was never discussed, so I will never know. What I do know is that she sought attention ceaselessly and loudly, gambled recklessly and may have been very unhappy. I loved her, yet did not altogether approve of the type of person she was.

There is no doubt in my mind that, had she tried to take us away and escape from my father, he would have pursued her relentlessly and perpetrated some unimaginable punishment upon her. Because that was one of the strange anomalies about this seemingly loving and normal father (which showed itself through my protecting wall): he was ruthlessly vindictive. No matter what I did, if my father disapproved of it, eventually he would be sure to 'get' me for it.

The sense of being constantly under threat hung over my whole life. I remembered at five years of age walking home from school and finding a mud puddle on the way. I had the most delightful time stamping in it, watching with sheer joy as brown slushy water shot out from under my shoes, splattering my clothes and squelching back over each foot as it sank in the mud. What marvellous fun! When my father saw those shoes, he turned on me with an expression near to loathing.

'Every week I clean these shoes for you, you good-for-nothing guttersnipe,' he snapped. 'I'll get you for this – you'll pay!' It took him six months to think up something vile enough to appease his need for retribution.

One of his favourite expressions seemed to be 'you'll pay!' or 'they'll pay!', used about all sorts of people and situations. I was not quite sure what it meant, but was to learn over the

years that he would bide his time until he found a punishment which he considered appropriate to justify the slight he
believed (rightly or wrongly) had been perpetrated upon
him. He never forgot, even if it took years to take vengeance,
and I never knew him to forgive.

Though I found it hard to reconcile these strange, cruel
quirks in his nature, I adored him. This has only added to
the incongruities in my mind. I know he punished us
severely for naughtiness or mistakes but, if we did something
well, this necessitated an even more merciless punishment. I
never understood his reasons for this; I just knew that was
how we functioned in our house. He frequently beat us and
felt quite justified in this as he told me often. 'My mother
died when I was three,' he would say, 'and Auntie So and
So, who brought us all up, beat me every day just for
exercise.' I have discovered since from a reliable source that
there was very little, if any truth in this statement. Yet he
believed it.

What made him like he was? What had produced this
man who could be so contradictory, for he seemed to derive
the most extraordinary pleasure from both hurting and
loving me?

Father was constantly changing his mind. He made
promises or gave permission for Clare or me to go somewhere and then refused to let us go. On several occasions
this happened as we were actually leaving the house. Or,
apparently full of concern, he would inquire why we were
not attending a certain function which he had previously
forbidden, when it was just too late for us to go. This kept
us in a perpetual state of indecision.

My parents never appeared to disagree in our presence,
though I've since remembered them shrieking abuse at each
other in private. Mother talked a lot and Father argued
constantly about his pet hate of the moment. His bigotry was
wide-ranging, particularly towards religion and other races.
His loathing for governments and neighbours, and especially

relatives, knew no bounds and his denunciation of the views of others on any topic was consistent: 'they' were always wrong!

By the time I was in the middle teens, I had grown to dislike him immensely, as many teenagers do with their parents. At times, as I struggled to gain some independence or put forward some observation I thought interesting, he would scoff loudly and, looking down from his full six feet three inches (190 cms), would snap out just one word – 'Tripe!'

Daily he insisted on walking with me to the station on our way to work while he pontificated on many matters. These conversations were mostly one-sided as I was usually breathless, trying to keep up with his long strides, and I'd learnt years ago not to butt in or disagree. One morning, as I puffed up the hill still listening, I felt deliciously diverted. A white van rattled past. Printed boldly on its side was just one word: 'Tripe'!

Father seemed to have a need to belittle others. I remember, with sickening recoil, having him poke his fingers into my ears, up my nose, into my eyes and scraping around the roof of my mouth with them, searching for my brains, as he explained between guffaws of laughter from him and my mother. Then triumphantly he'd shout for all to hear that he hadn't found any brains inside Cathy Ann's head.

My mortification at that time was unbearable, but worst of all was the fact that all through my life I carried the belief that I must be utterly stupid, because my daddy hadn't found my brains. Six years ago, I needed to have a catscan and there they were – my brains – completely visible. Like a child with a present, I ran around poking that X-ray under the noses of Rob and my children, absolutely delighted to show them my brains. No-one really understood my ridiculous elation.

I grew to love Dad again in my twenties, though once he told me that if ever I wanted something from him, he would make sure he never gave it to me. How strange from a father who said he loved me! Yet this was nothing to the horrors I was discovering now, the awful repressed secrets which were being revealed to my conscious mind. I found it all beyond my comprehension to understand.

Why? Why me? Why did my father have to be such a fiend when I loved him so much?

Where was my beautiful, happy childhood picture? Shattered!

What would fill its place now?

Clare, knowing the facts, gently tried to prepare me. 'You've only just seen the tip of the iceberg; you've only seen a tiny part of what our parents did to us!' she told me quietly.

'Oh no, not more!'

4

The spider hunt

HOW PLEASANT IT WAS in the garden. I was enjoying loafing on the grass, trimming the edge of the path. Just doing something physical and not emotionally demanding, after the strain of the last few months, was very relaxing.

Glancing down, I noticed the grass had left its intricate pattern on my leg.

'Can you see those funny criss-crossy marks on my leg, dolly, Blue Bell? Now that I have dressed you and stood up to take you for your walk, I can see them. It's all right – they're only the grass I was sitting on. It was all prickly, but I don't mind, 'cause it's nice out here in our garden with you and the sun's so warm.'

Clare has just started school and she is practising her reading on the back verandah. Mummy said I am going to school in a year or so when I turn five. Then I will be able to read, too. I think Mummy's inside our house and I can see Daddy. He's coming across the grass in his garden clothes from the dark side of the house where all the ferns grow.

'Hello Cathy Ann, what are you doing?'

'I'm taking Blue Bell for a walk in her pram, Daddy.'

My daddy's very, very big, and I like him. Just sometimes I see a funny sort of look on his face. I don't like that daddy: that's not my real daddy. He's that bad daddy who is here sometimes. He's here now! I'll take dolly. I'll move away. I'm frightened of that daddy. Oh no! He's leaning over me.

'Look out, Cathy Ann, there's a spider on you!'
'Where? Where? Get it off. No, not a spider! I can feel it crawling on me!'
'Daddy will get it for you, Annie. I'll get it.'
'It's not down there, Daddy. I can feel it up higher, round my middle. Please, Daddy, don't do that. Please find the spider. Don't laugh at me like that, Daddy. I don't think it's funny. I don't like spiders. Oh, please take it out!' I think my daddy put that spider down my dress so he could look for it.
'Why would you do that to me, Daddy?'

It's all coming back to me now. He was 'setting me up' for later.

Often when my childhood repressions burst unheralded upon me, they overwhelm me with the same intensity and utter reality experienced in a nightmare. As though it's all happening at that very moment, I see, I participate – my whole being is involved. Every emotion is entered into with heightened awareness. Pain hurts. Frustration consumes in its vehemence. My anger rises. Fear clutches my throat. My heart pounds in terror. Arms flay, striving to ward off danger, as my legs struggle to escape, yet cannot.

Each emotion is acutely real, the pictures vivid, believable, believed – the actual happenings flashing into my conscious mind with the violent force of the original encounter. I rediscover the hidden episodes of my childhood. I relive each emotion to its fullest, as a fifty-year-old adult. Yet, unlike in a nightmare, I am completely aware of being in the now: surroundings, companions, everything. Sometimes I can even withdraw from my experience and then re-enter it.

So now, after reliving my revulsion at having that spider down my clothing, I am beginning to realise that it wasn't just for his own 'fun' that my father played his sadistic tricks upon us. He had a purpose: his own deviant need for sexual stimulation. I had been dreading making this discovery which I felt sure must be repressed in my memories: his sexual violation of me.

Only yesterday I had remembered the spider episode and knew the rest of it would come back to me in time. And this morning I have been plunged into the nightmare of my very early childhood. The sun has just broken through grey clouds and the dawn light is throwing back the night's darkness. But not in my soul! In me is fear, isolation, pain and a fierce anger. For again I am reliving a shocking memory of being only a little toddler and already the victim of that man's warped mind.

I hurt and I'm afraid. Why doesn't someone help me? I feel utterly alone. Who cares? No-one cares. No-one. . . Not even God. Where are you, God? How could God allow a thing like this to happen to anyone, especially two lovely little girls. . . Clare and that dear little baby girl? Me! *Me!*

I don't want it to have happened to me. I don't want it to have been me. No, I can't take that. It's too painful. I'll not remember it happening to me. I'll not believe it happened to me. Did it? That little thing cringing in terror trying to hide in the corner of the bed, hard up against the wall: is that me? With that hurting up inside me from Daddy's thumb?

I'm so frightened. I can see me, so very young, holding myself up as straight as I can, 'cause if I fall forward, Daddy's nail might cut right through me. It's so high up here, hoisted up on Daddy's thumb.

'Oh please put me down, Daddy. Don't laugh, Daddy, stop, stop. Oh please put me down!' Is that Mummy's voice?
'Don't do that, Henry, I don't think that's good for her holding her up like that, though she does look so funny trying to keep up straight! Look out, I think she's going to be sick. Stop that, you disgusting child!'
'Oh, Mummy, I thought you were coming to help me.'
No-one comes to help me. What can I do? Just die, because of the pain and fear. But I'm not dying, I'm going on living. What if Daddy does it again – or something else, something worse?

I don't want to remember. I won't remember. I'll forget it and put it away somewhere and never look at it again. That's the best thing to do. I'll act like it never happened and be extra nice to Mummy and Daddy and accept whatever they do to me. I'll get loved that way and maybe it won't happen again.

This was the decision I believe I made at an early age. Not that I had any control over the results of it, nor that I made it altogether in my conscious mind. Yet, little as I understand it, I know I made that decision and many others just to stay alive and cope. I made this resolution to do the very best I could for myself in the circumstances and it keeps on recurring all through my life. I call it my 'best person to be' and, unless God steps in and overrules it and substitutes something better, I fear I will go on using it as long as I live.

This morning, fifty years later, the fear and humiliation have turned to anger. How could they have violated me so? How could anyone treat a little child like that? Their own child! And why? Why me? Why didn't someone help? Why didn't God help? I don't understand. I just don't know what to think.

Perhaps God doesn't love me, like my parents didn't. So why would he help me if he didn't love me? I know what it is! God didn't love me and take care of me because I am awful and just not lovable. If I were lovable, my parents would have loved me and not treated me like that. I want them to love me. They have to love me, have to. If they don't I will go mad.

It's strange how, even as a middle-aged woman, I can slip back, so simply, into my childhood needs. All the love from Robert and my children and friends has not compensated for my parents' failure to love and accept me. Sadly, the love I have received since has not overcome that initial need. It doesn't matter how often I am told I am loved, how often I am shown love and care, how often people try to boost my ego or change my thinking by telling me nice things about myself. Even if I know they are true, nothing alters my original concepts about myself. I still believe about myself what I have always believed.

Recently I read an intuitive statement: 'They told me fish cared very little. . . were cold-blooded and felt no pain. But they were not fish who told me.' In these words I perceived a truth. What others say doesn't alter what I know inside myself, for no matter how much affirmation others so lovingly give me, my original picture remains unchanged, an intrinsic part of me. . . I feel unwanted, unlovable, worthless.

This heartbreaking knowledge is the reference point on which I have built my whole concept of myself. These were the messages I received from my earliest perceptions, including the failure of my parents' attempts to abort me. My mother told me about that. I have no reference point of nurture from loving parents, nor of their concern for me as a person in my own right. I do not seem to have been considered as a human being of the slightest value, except as a victim – some sort of unfeeling recipient for their anger and lusts. When they wanted something from me they were loving and in front of other people they appeared as fond, caring parents. This only added confusion to my heartache, for how I longed to believe them!

The rejection of my parents has caused me a lifetime of suffering. It is not just the cruelty, mental and physical, which they perpetrated upon me, the pain and anguish of which was hard enough to bear. More serious was that I had decided the cause of it all must be my own basic, innate badness which aroused in them such repugnance that it caused them to reject me. This knowledge, whether true or false, has gripped my life, undermining everything I have tried to do, colouring every achievement with a grey wash of failure.

Being a loving, helpful wife and companion to my husband and the caring, though far-from-perfect, mother of my three much-loved children had not been able to assuage my rejection of myself, nor that of my parents.

I cannot help but wonder if there is the slightest point to my existence. A desire to escape, to no longer exist, in fact even to die rather than live one moment more with that indescribable anguish gnawing at the very heart of my being, often seeks to overwhelm me. For I see it as a whole life undermined, defeated, useless, hopelessly wasted. Is this true? Those who love me try to assure me it is not so.

It seems obvious that for me no human intervention can heal the aching wound left by parental rejection or heal scars so deep, hurts so intense. Can God?

I knew there was a God. I believed that. Even if I was not always sure of his love for me and was frequently opposed to him, I believe that somehow, some way, he has enabled me to cope. A burning desire to believe and trust him has added a tenacity to my struggle to know him, to try to understand why he allowed the horror of my childhood.

But I have real difficulties: my fight is to believe that God is strong, reliable, kind and just, in spite of the scream within me which denies this.

My forgetting place

Always it is quiet here.
Here is somewhere safe to come
to my log.
No-one else sits on it,
behind the big locked gate
and tall paling fence.
Sometimes cows come here,
but children don't and I am glad.
Because I can come and be here
by myself.

It 's quiet here.
Here is where I do my forgetting.
About last night,
that awful thing my daddy did
in bed again.
And Mummy screaming –
how she hates me so.
I touch my log;
it knows I hurt.
'Do you, God?'

It's quiet here.
Here is where I hide it all away
inside me.
Here stills the sad that's in me.
I can go home now
to face their love and
face their hate.
I'll climb up over the big locked gate.
It's not so hard, now that
I am nearly eight.

5

The family dinner

TODAY WHAT JOY! I woke feeling happy. There is not a low in my mood, nor an excessive high. Just a level, a plateau. Who could have believed that such a pleasant place existed and that I, of the deep troughs of depression or the fleeting meteoric heights of exultation, could be lying here enjoying such peace and quietness of spirit.

'Hurrah!' I feel like cheering. For today I am not weighed down by my own personal accuser, not troubled by the guilt and self-condemnation which are often my first thoughts for each new day. Usually I blame myself for having harmed a loved one, heaping scorn and bitterness upon myself, often without even knowing why. Ah! but not today. In fact, a great day for golf. I haven't played for years: I never was any good at sport. I remember though, just once, I won a prize for golf: 'The most number of strokes for a hole,' the ticket said.

It still makes me chortle: I haven't had a good laugh for months. Not too much to laugh about, with all the worries about the children and the anguish caused by my memories from my childhood. Also, going every week to my counsellor knocks me about. She's marvellously kind and skilled, but it takes all the courage I can dig up to go and face those awful discoveries. In fact, the pain and isolation I feel afterwards are so intense that it can take days to recover. At her suggestion, I have agreed to see a psychiatrist in another state, one who specialises in helping the victims of childhood abuse.

Anyway, no more fretting, for today is special and I intend to luxuriate in the joy of feeling happy, because tonight all the family will be here for dinner – that's good! I'll set the table now, so I can spend the rest of the day preparing. That cream tablecloth looks right, with the floral place mats Grace gave me. Tonight's dinner is especially for her, a farewell.

Oh, how I wish you weren't going, Grace 'me darling'. It's not that I mind you travelling – we all love that – but hitchhiking around Asia! You're only twenty. I'm scared for you. I've tried every way I know to persuade you to travel some other way. All right, no money! You're so adamant. How can someone so slender, so fragile-looking, be so determined? I will seat you next to your dad tonight, though I'd rather you were sitting beside me. I want to keep you close, as if I could protect you by that. I know you have learnt to be independent since you moved out a year ago, but you're still my 'little girl' and hitchhiking in Asia is so dangerous! I've told you all the dangers I can think of.

'Oh Mum! You worry too much,' you said. 'You're just being a clucky mum.'

Guess I have overdone that side of it. But that's me – worrying again, not trusting. I've tried to trust God and prayed lots about the whole trip, but I'm still not convinced God will look after you. However, I will follow the good advice my friend Ellen gave me: 'Try to understand that Grace needs to go and wants to do it her way. Send her with your love and blessing,' she said.

We all want you to have a fabulous time, Grace. I guess it's not easy for you leaving the job you like so much. I realise now, better than ever before, that when you have to do something, you just have to. I'm glad you're travelling with Kelly. We like her and she will be a great companion: reliable and very protective. Does God have a sense of humour? I'm sure of it. He has fascinating ways of saying, 'Learn to trust me!' For Kelly, even though she may be twenty-seven and much travelled, is only four feet eleven inches (151 cms) tall!

You always were adventurous, my sweet Grace. An interesting child, unusual, independent, a lateral thinker, intelligent and gentle. How we laughed at those hilariously funny things you said as a child, yet with a touch of sharpness to your humour. It always was your defence against Bart. He might be three years younger, but he had the brawn and always wanted to fight you physically. I know your remarks made him furious on occasions.

I hope we all keep our cool tonight. You say you will be back in a year – that's a long time and so much can happen. Well, I can only try to trust God to look after you. 'Oh Lord, please keep her safe and bring her home so we can all be together again for Sarah's wedding.'

Sarah getting married! How exciting! 'This is my wedding, Mum,' you said. 'I want to arrange it all myself.'

What a relief. I was dreading having to cope with all the arrangements. Thanks, Sarah. You have always been so capable, using your talents in your profession, helping people so much. It'll be an absolutely terrific wedding. Dear vital Sarah, of the honesty and sudden mood swings; Sarah, rushing out some mornings shouting, 'Don't speak to me anyone. I'm in a lousy mood.'

Tonight, you can sit on the other side of your dad. I'm glad you've come home again to live; we should be able to patch up the holes in our relationship now we've both survived your teen years. I guess you were just growing up and I panicked when you began to change. If I hadn't taken it all so seriously and been so uptight, you would not have needed to swing so far out to find your own individuality. You had to fight every step of the way.

Oh, the awful arguments your dad, you and I had, while I hung on like grim death for fear of losing you, driving you further away. I wish I had trusted your innate sense of what was right, that goodness inside you and our years of teaching you about Christ's principles – and our daily prayers for you. These should have enabled me to let you go. And, to be honest, I suppose they should have helped you not to be quite so intent on living how you wanted. It's lovely to see you sorting yourself out, so let's relax with each other now and enjoy this year together.

I like your young man. (Gosh, husband-to-be! Must get used to that.) He's nice – seems very dependable and I know you're making your choice after much prayer and thought.

'He meets my emotional needs, Mum,' you said. Here's wisdom beyond your years. Wisdom. . . that's what we all need in dealing with each other. I certainly need wisdom with Bart. 'There's no point in getting all worked up now, Ann. Just set his place at the table and pray.'

My dear son, Bart. You're very sensitive. I wish you didn't feel you have to hide it by being extra tough. You really have so much potential, so much going for you. Don't waste it. I notice you have suddenly grown so tall but thin, too thin. I worry about you. It's the life you're leading, not eating proper meals and staying out all night. People say, 'Oh, it's just teenage boys; he's only seventeen and finding his feet!' I fear you are going down a path which isn't safe for you, but you won't listen to us. We pray so much for you.

I don't like the way you are living, Bart. I don't know whether you'll come in for dinner tonight or not. You said you would, but you don't always do as you say. If you do, will you be all right, or will you be distant, sullen, wanting to dash off as soon as you can? Maybe you'll be your old loving self, warm and considerate, telling us those crazy jokes you do so well. I think underneath you are hurting very much. You can sit beside me tonight and we'll enjoy a laugh together.

It all worries your dad, too. I know it's not easy for you,

Rob, constantly caring for people in every avenue of their lives. So many pressures and so much expected of you and of us, too; I think clergy families sometimes get it extra hard. The children's contemporaries seem to make fun of them. Does it make them have to prove something to the world that perhaps other kids don't need to?

I feel that pressure, too, as though it's necessary to present this facade of us all coping in an expected 'Christian' way. I guess it makes it more difficult for you, Rob. I wonder if it feels as though the world is watching to see if you are performing the way they think a clergyman should?

Unfortunately, we have expectations of you as well. We want you to have all the answers and help us, too. It's been a heavy load, especially with me having that unexplained depression over the years. Having to go away so often in your job – sometimes home, sometimes not – has in many ways made our lives much harder, I think.

Those times you were gone for six month stints were really difficult. We found functioning without you was never easy, but we'd grow accustomed to it. Then you'd return and the family's way of coping would alter again. Confusing for the children, especially where discipline was concerned when they were younger. For me, your returns would bring much pleasure, but there was always sorting out to do.

Rob, my dear, I think you work too hard, though I really do enjoy being involved in it with you. Many of the twenty or so moves we had were difficult and some of the places we've lived in have been more challenging than others. I've always enjoyed the ones where we've had 'open house'. Having Bible studies in the home and lots of people and meetings kept me busy. That's why I've appreciated all the help from you and the family. It enabled me to cope and also join a few groups for arts and crafts and reading, special things which I enjoy.

Remember, years ago, how that friend in the reading group tried to shock me every night, saying those really provocative things and swearing like a trooper? She did wonders for me to get me out of my prim ways. Later, she told me how amused she was to see me blush. How times have changed!

Will the children swear over dinner tonight, I wonder? Are they just teasing me, trying to get me to be a bit less proper and rigid? Could be, or it might be just their oddball sense of humour! Funny – it's just hit me. I've never remembered before how disgustingly my father used to swear in private when he was angry. Strange how the return of a memory like that can explain a whole reason why I have reacted in a certain way. I'd better get on with this table-setting job.

We are changing though, Robby. I guess the family growing up is changing us, as well as my childhood coming out into the open. Thanks for being so patient and standing by me through it all. I really appreciate that. It's difficult for anyone to know how to help, but I love you for trying. I wouldn't blame you if all the suffering in our lives, at the moment, made you want to retreat into your work. Yet I know you long to help us and hold on to us. So thanks for praying and for your faith in God through it all.

The dinner party was just great! I needn't have worried. We all enjoyed being together. Rob was able to sit back and relax. Grace and Sarah were so excited about the trip and the wedding and Bart was full of fun, cracking lots of jokes with us all.

For me, it rounded out my happy day beautifully.

Where are you, God?

Where are you, God?
  I'd like to talk with you.
I wish I could find you
  so I can pray to you.
I need the contact of conversation,
  the lessons from listening.
Yet when I start, the words seem
  stereotyped – lifeless.
The phrases, hackneyed wordy cliches
  without sense. . . or purpose.

    Sometimes it feels as though I'm talking to
      no-one.
    That's all too unreal for me,
      God!
    Just so much pretence.

There is a way I want to pray. . .
I'd like to talk and
   share with you.
Even shout and argue,
   ask and cajole.
Whisper in reverence or
   yell in exuberance.
I want to be able to disagree,
   weep my sorrows,
Pour forth my complaints,
   open my heartaches.
Then gently delight in your companionship,
   thirsting for your promises,
   finding your encouragement.

   Just as if I'm talking to
      someone.
   That's more real for me,
      God!
   Not just pretence.

Enthusiastically seeking,
I'm back to the fray,
quesing and questioning.
Demanding, accusing,
struggling to comprehend.
Hopefully trusting,
acquiescing to your will.
Quietly waiting,
expecting your overruling.
Humbly sharing
even my disobedience.
Thankfully accepting
the wonder of your forgiveness.

Conversing with
you
as I've never spoken with another person,
God!
That's reality for me.

6

The two daddies

OH YES, THAT'S how I want to pray and sometimes I do, but often when I begin to pray I am brought to an abrupt halt, for fear, potent and consuming, stops me, clutching at my throat, drying up my words into brittle croakings of conventional barrenness. Such fear, holding my thoughts in a rigid pattern of repetitive cycles.

But why? As though in answer, emblazoned across my mind, come words from the Bible: 'Your God is a consuming fire.' What does this mean? Where is the loving God, the compassionate Father? How can I expose my soul to a Being who will consume me? Where is the safety of love? The mastery over fear? Nevertheless, I take courage and ask God what is his explanation of the fear which grips me when I want to talk with him.

Suddenly I slip back into a childhood memory and seem to see God high above me, apparently so removed – so pure, so indifferent to my pleas. Looking down with. . . is it disdain?. . . upon that weeping, battered child: me at only six years of age!

My skirt is on fire, smouldering, with little sparks flicking at my legs. I'm running, screaming, across the garden, through the open back gate. Can't get over the bar! Daddy's coming. . . *Run! Faster. . . Run.* I run into the paddock, through the bushes, but Daddy grabs me. Down onto the dirt. Daddy's beating out the fire. Beating me hard everywhere, even where there's no fire. Around my legs, shoulders, back. Kicking me and yelling, 'Must put out the fire!' Even though the fire's out. . . still beating.

I lie there, breathing smoke, dirt in my face, up my nose, down into my mouth, sticking to my tears and sweat in nasty brown globs. All over is pain.

I lift my head from the dust and twist my face upwards, raising my aching arm. I make a little fist and shake it at God, then, with a child's moan of despair, beg with all my heart: 'Look at me down here, God! All hurting and sore and frightened. My daddy did this to me and you just let him. Help me! If you don't, I'll never speak to you again. Please help me!'

I hear the people from the house next door rushing up. 'What happened? What happened?'

Daddy's voice: 'Poor little Annie got too close to the incinerator. I told her not to – her skirt caught on fire.'

Sobbing. In my mind I cry: 'No, it wasn't like that. Daddy took a roll of paper out of the incinerator. It was alight. He stretched his arm out towards me. . .

'Now fire is dangerous,' he says. 'Never play with fire because it burns. Ann, you need a lesson about fire.' Daddy, laughing, poking that fire at my legs and up under my skirt. I'm backing away – I've had lessons like this before.

I remember doing something really well and hoping for a little praise. Then the words from Daddy: 'You are so proud. I will stop you from being proud and deflate your pride, my girl.' He's sticking pins in me, down my fingernails. 'This will teach you a lesson not to be proud.'

I know about Daddy's lessons, so must get away before. . . too late! My legs are burning, my skirt's on fire. . . panic, screaming, running, gasping for breath. I'm caught. . . I'm falling.

I can hear Daddy's voice explaining. 'I had to stop her and roll her on the ground to beat out the fire. Come to Daddy, Annie, my poor girlie. Don't cry! It's all right, Daddy's here.' He's lifting me, cuddling me. Yes, Daddy is here. But Daddy cannot be trusted. Daddy is really two daddies: one loving, one awful and cruel. Two daddies!

Somehow, some way, I make a jump in my mind – to God. Are there two Gods: one loving, one a consuming fire? Do I equate God with my father? Did I make a childhood decision that God was like, even the same as my father? Is God synonymous in my mind with that cruel, capricious man: one moment loving with Clare and me, the next torturing us with sadistic pleasure and ruling us with impossible discipline? Supposedly reliable, yet never to be trusted. Always I must be on guard, constantly alert to every mood, aware of the slightest change in his approach. Yet it was impossible to be prepared for his next attack.

Have I believed these things about God? I always thought of my father as God. He was God to me. He was my only model. Who else could I look to, so that I could understand what a Father God was like? But I was wrong. *God and my father are not the same.* The fire my father subjected me to could have destroyed me. I can now start to believe that God's fire is cleansing and purifying, and it separates – yet not without pain, the worth from the worthless in me, burning up the rubbish, opening up a whole new life.

It reminds me of fires in the Australian bush, their very intensity bursting open the pods of the banksia trees to enable the seeds to break free and grow in the fertile ash left in their wake. I can now begin to trust that God is somehow like that – working in my life, setting me free to start again, to grow in new ways, to regenerate, to become a different person from the one so hurt by my childhood. I delight in these revelations. Here are warm, healing discoveries. God and my father are not the same. I do not have to fear him any more. It was really my father I feared and I transferred this to how I felt about God.

It was my father who hurt me. He seemed to drag me through a door in that invisible wall which had partitioned off my life. It was in that place, which I am now finding the courage to enter, that his needs had to be met by me. For it was there he violated my privacy and there he used me for his gratification, making me feel like a thing.

It was all there stored away: how I had to meet his sexual desires and cheer him up if he was sad; how he would vent his spleen in beating us until his fierce anger had abated. I had to satisfy his sadistic urges which seemed to alleviate some weird, mental aberration that made him outwardly extraordinarily puritanical. He blamed me for his behaviour, saying I was wicked and evil and it was this very wickedness which drove him to his deviant activities.

I believed him. What else could I do? If my much-loved daddy said I was evil, then I must be. He should know. He lived with me; he punished me for it often enough.

At last I am beginning to see that my father was not the good daddy I had thought for so long. Now that the door has been flung open in my mind allowing the truth to be seen, I do not have to cringe in fear of God or hate him instead of my father. Nor do I need to have my 'antennas' always out, scanning others to ascertain if I am safe. Now that I have made these restoring discoveries I can look further into my life. There is still more truth to know and more healing to come from that knowing.

I have now honestly to face my doubts about God in other areas of my life. A friend said once, 'Discontent is the fuel of victory.' These words have spurred me on. A statement by John Donne – 'Would you know the truth? Doubt, and then you will inquire' – has shown me that others also have doubts.

And the words taken from Unamuno's *The Tragic Sense of Life* have fired some profound response in me, though I do not agree with them entirely: 'Those who believe they believe in God, but without passion in the heart, without anguish of mind, without uncertainty, without doubt and even, at times, without despair, believe only in the idea of God and not in God himself.'

Yes, there is still anguish of mind, uncertainty, doubt.

How I have doubted. How I have questioned and demanded answers from God, answers to the suffering of my childhood and the suffering this has produced in Robert, Sarah, Grace and Bart, answers to the suffering of others the world over.

Has God answered? Sometimes, assuredly. Especially when my anger has been at its height or my belief at its lowest and my faith at the limit of its extremities. It is at these times, when I have been too scared to trust him and too afraid not to, that I have asked him to step in and manage that very lack of trust.

But I am only just beginning to learn these lessons of having God overrule in my life. More often, I wonder, if I acknowledge my doubts, will God pour down fire and brimstone on me? If I tell him truly how I feel about him and what I am really like, will he punish me? Or will he know that this is my confession, sharing with him the very truth of who I really am, with all my doubts, fears and even hatred – and the guilt these cause?

I can start to comprehend that it is the rebellious, doubting and angry person, also that hurt little child in me, that God longs to speak with and have me surrender to him; not that proper religious me I've tried so hard to present over all these years. Not the person who thought God would only like me if I was good. That's not the real me.

I want to believe that God cares about the real me. For I am convinced that unless he comes back into my past with me, unless he does the healing, unless he works his active forgiveness within me and alters my perception and adapting, all the reliving and comprehending will be for nothing.

7

The heartbreaking secret

'WHAT'S YOUR SECRET?' I stood and stared uncomprehend-ingly at the friend opposite me in the small group we'd just joined. My heart gave a jump and began to pound, my stomach constricted, as panic tried to send me racing back out of that room.

'Come on now, Cathy Ann,' he insisted, 'what's your secret?' Did he really want to know my secrets, those fearful things which lay hidden inside me?

Within the briefest second I took in the scene: the large, beautiful old room, dark-panelled walls with their soft patina, reflecting the men resplendent in their evening suits, the women, splashes of colour – a touch of movie magic. It always filled me with delight, though we came here frequent-ly to dine or for formal occasions. It was all part of Robert's life, one of the social aspects of his professional duties, and I loved it; all the fun of dressing up and being waited on during a gracious meal. I called it 'playing ladies'.

Now I studied this small group: some strangers, a few we knew well; and Tom, who'd spoken, and his wife – both close friends. Diana moved towards me with a welcoming kiss. 'Now look here,' Tom pressed on, 'I haven't seen you for months and you look even younger. We all want to know your secret.'

Relief! I kissed Diana back with extra warmth. The relief!

I laughed and tossed off a flippant remark to Tom about losing weight, damped down the fear of exposure rising in me and smiled my biggest smile. Holding on to Diana's hand secretly for support, I asked about her family and what were they doing these days?

My eyes roved around that pleasant gathering. Could anyone there guess what was happening inside me? I thought not. I was introduced to others and began a light conversation with a weekend farmer on, of all topics, battery chickens – and the evening was away. . . I'd come through.

It's moments like these that I need the training of all those years behind me: of hiding my feelings, of being able to put on my most pleasant face and move into what has become, for me, my safety zone – that place of pretending that I can cope in the ordinary, normal, everyday world. There is no way I could exist, mentally or emotionally, if I had to live every day being always conscious of that terrible childhood which I was now just beginning to allow out of its repressed place.

Hence my panic in case this was the secret Tom had discovered. This would, indeed, have set the cat among the battery chickens.

Frequently I find it disturbing that, while one part of me is enjoying an activity, another part is filled with a sense of inferiority, as though everyone else there is nicer, kinder, more capable and much more clever than me – in fact all topnotch achievers! Funny thing is no-one ever seems to notice I am below par.

There's a certain irony in all this for me. Sometimes I've noticed that when I'm feeling my internal pain most severely I tend to look shocking, which seems completely appropriate. But the strange thing is that there are also occasions, like tonight, when just the opposite takes place and, after a week of heartbreaking discoveries, oddly I look outwardly more alive, more healthy and more attractive.

This experience is confusing and threatening for me, because my internal state and my external appearance do not coincide. My outward self tells a story which is only a small part of my whole picture, for it expresses serenity, warmth, friendliness and glimmers of fun. It makes me feel a hypocrite.

Yet that's how I cope. By making my appearance as attractive as possible (given the original material provided), I cope by hiding how I really feel and by pretending. But it's not just pretence. The teenage self within me tells me there's a reason. If I look really attractive my dad won't touch me, so to take special care of my appearance is a defence for me. It keeps Dad at bay; he won't hit me or mess me up if he likes how I look. I have to try to please him to keep safe.

I don't mean to pretend; it just happens. I don't produce it in any way. It seems to be an automatic behavioural pattern I've built up – maybe what the experts call a defence mechanism. It has been necessary to pretend that I was all right on the surface. It's the way I hid all the pain I had in the past and the same way, now, I'm hiding the pain I'm reliving.

It's not only the remembering that's so devastating; it is the reliving, in their extraordinary intensity, the emotions of those repressed traumas. I am enduring many hours of pain, filled with new and more terrible disclosures. There are nights of horrible revelations, days of staggering blindly about the house — clutching doorways, collapsing against walls, onto floors — with soul-searing hurt and pain dredging up from the very depths of my being, making sounds I cannot bear to hear, music playing so loudly to hide those awful screaming laments: Rachmaninov's Concerto No. 2 in C minor played over and over, or jazz blaring through the house.

I am discovering about my father's cruelty, my mother's collaboration.

Externally, I'm not very different from the others there. The distressing thing for me is. . . I feel different! For just below that pleasant exterior, which matches theirs, is the unshakable knowledge that I am really no good and not fit to mix with them.

'Ann, Cathy Ann!' Diana's voice broke into my thoughts. 'Let's go and powder our noses.' Diana and another guest began a lengthy conversation. I moved to the mirror, smiling at a few friends I knew. I wonder why those mirrors are always so revealing? I stood staring at myself, suddenly stunned by the resemblance to my mother.

My mother! What had been her part in my past? I had wondered that ever since the true – though still hard-to-believe – facts of my childhood had been revealed to me. Now I knew at least some of her collaboration in that abusing. Yes, only last week I had made that discovery.

I had remembered not being very well at school all one day when I was about eight. I'd had an awful fright the night before when I'd woken abruptly with a sharp pain in my shoulder. It was my daddy. He'd thrown back the bedclothes and clamped his whole mouth over my shoulder. This daddy was not my nice daddy. It was that horrible daddy who came into my life often. He whispered to me. . .

'Let Daddy play with you, Annie.'
Scared and still mainly asleep, I begged: 'No, Daddy, please no!'
He opened his mouth wide again and grabbed my little throat in it. 'If you don't let Daddy, I'll bite right through your throat and the blood will gush out and you'll die slowly and horribly.' He had his way. . . he sexually violated me.
Clare and I had got ourselves off to school the next morning; Mummy didn't always get up. Somehow I'd scraped through that day and come home to Mummy as quickly as I could. I needed her to love and help me. When I ran into the kitchen, she was ironing.
'Mummy, I feel sick,' I blurted out.
She just raised her head and stared at me with a cold, hard look on her face. Snatching up the iron, she lunged towards

me. I staggered back. She pushed it close to my face. It was so hot! Quickly she stopped.

'If I put this iron on your face, like I should,' she said, 'all the marks will show and people will know. Come over here, Cathy Ann. Do as you are told. Put your hands down on the table.' She slammed that hot iron down on to the backs of my hands. Later she told others, 'That stupid child poured hot water all over her hands.'

Oh Mummy! I needed you so much just to love me, not to hurt me more. . .

I stared into that mirror. Had any of those ladies at that very pleasant party noticed any change in me? Apparently not. But when I'd met Clare last week, she had noticed that something worse had come back to my memory. We talked more about Mother's part in our childhood. As always, Clare was understanding and felt for me. Yet she took what I shared calmly, quite matter-of-fact. It fascinates me how much we can find to laugh about in it all when we are together. I had recalled an episode in our kitchen. . .

I've never liked the smell of gas. It nauseates both Clare and me. I'm not surprised now! I had remembered one of those awful fights, with Mummy yelling and pushing Clare's head into the oven of our gas stove, and Clare struggling and fighting, and me pulling and trying to drag Mummy off. Mummy was so strong, she just threw me aside as though I wasn't even there. Crash! My head slammed into the corner of the little cupboard under the mirror, the blood running all down my face. Mummy shrieked and let Clare go. I actually felt the physical pain of it and the cloying smell of gas in the reliving of the memory.

Poor Clare! Still, she seems so at peace. 'I've handed it all over to God,' she said. 'It's all in the past.' As though it had happened to two other people. Thanks for your faith, Clare. I can hold on to that, too, and believe that God will bring me through sane. Not unscarred, but sane.

'I can understand now why you hate gas stoves so much,' I said. 'I could never work it out before.'

'I guess,' said Clare with a grin, 'I've had my head shoved in them too often to really appreciate them.'

The party, at last, was drawing to a close and I was relieved. Maintaining my 'front' had been using up enormous amounts of my small stock of energy. Pretending again? When I have to, I cope; it's afterwards I am exhausted. When I am home, that's when I flop – drained of any coping ability, no longer able to pretend, dragging from one household chore to another, my weariness made more severe by that 'little abused girl' erupting out of my childhood. Tessa my counsellor had gently explained that I must give myself permission to believe the sufferings of my childhood, that I must begin to take care of that 'little girl' inside me who only wanted to be loved and was not.

Now I was remembering, as well, that my mother did not love me. As I grew into my early teens her anger also grew, spurred on, I discovered later, by her secret drinking. Perhaps she could not have coped otherwise. . .

One Sunday morning, after my father had raped me during the previous night (I cannot, even now, make that statement easily; to talk about it is still immensely difficult for me), I came slowly, heavily out to the kitchen. Mum was slicing bread for toast with a long, sharp knife. As I approached, she swung round fast and grabbed my hair. The knife came up and across my throat. (Incredibly, though true, I can feel it even now!)

'Mum! Why! What are you doing?' She is holding me by the hair, glaring into my eyes with a strange look on her face and it's all red and puffy. Her eyes are two tiny dots.

'You filthy slut!' Somehow her voice sounds thick and hoarse, not like it usually is when she sings around the house, or when she's talking to visitors; then it's a nice musical voice.

'You filthy little slut!' she seems to hiss.

Why is Mum holding that knife at my throat? What have I

done? What is a slut? Is it because of last night? Was that all my fault because I am so evil, because I know that sometimes when Dad touches me he seems to make me feel as though it's pleasant for me, though I really hate it? Is that what a slut is? Is that why Mum is so terribly angry?

Confusion, thoughts, words, fear all jumbled up together. I'm scared, too afraid to try to escape, just standing there, deathly still, smelling that sweet, sickly smell of wine. Is Mum going to cut my throat and kill me? No; somehow I know she won't kill me, but she could easily hurt me.

Slowly she lowers the knife from my throat. She's still holding my hair hard and tight in her other hand, and breathing very heavily, staring all about, quivering. 'If your father comes into bed again with you, I'll. . . I'll. . . each time I'll chop off one of your fingers, just like a carrot! So you keep him out. Do you hear me? Keep him out!'

Oh yes, I hear you, my mum, my lovely mum. But he's such a great big man. How can I keep him out, how can I?

Even though Clare is only eighteen months older than me, I remember she was always very kind. Again she helped me that day and we got ready to go to Sunday school. We'd been going there most Sundays since I was three and it was a special place for us. Clare was learning to teach Sunday school when she turned fifteen.

That day there was no reason we would want to hurry home, so we stayed on for the church service. They sang an old hymn with one verse based on God's promises in the Bible – from Isaiah, chapter 49:

> *Can a mother's tender care*
> *Cease towards the child she bare?*
> *Yes, she may forgetful be.*
> *Yet will I remember thee.*

New day

Often have I waited,
watching for the morning.
Seeking courage,
as that first inflow of light
absorbs the darkness.
Highlighting before me
shapes,
dimly grey-bulked,
monotonously dull.
Transforming all into another dimension.
Evolving from drabness God's gift for my new day.
Colour.

Exciting my eyes,
  seeping into my soul.
Giving me courage,
  after sleepless nights
    of prayerful weeping.
Bursting before me
  shades,
    exquisitely blended,
      vibrantly alive.
Transforming all with limitless variety.
Evoked from the depths of God's profound resources.
  Colour.

8

The cushion room

AT LAST I WAS HERE! Rob had taken me to the interstate bus early yesterday morning and I remember his look of deep concern and uncertainty. We were both apprehensive about this trip to the psychiatrist, Dr David, but my counsellor, Tessa, had advised me to see him as he worked extensively helping people in trauma.

Surprisingly, his rambling old house was much in need of care and attention, its garden drab and unkempt. Yet to enter was for me to be freed from the conventionalities: the floors with their scruffy worn carpets were scattered with rugs, some old, some lovely, beautifully textured and patterned; paint needed here and there, cracking walls making the corners slightly askew; high ceilings, ornate flaking.

Above the verandah door a large multi-coloured cellophane fish swam languidly in the breeze, while a friendly golden labrador ambled over to greet me. Scores of pictures and huge screen-printed hangings of trees and leafy traceries filled the rooms, making each unique. Prisms at the windows caught the sunlight and flung the rainbow unexpectedly and indiscriminately over people and objects, falling on lovely old furniture, comfortably moulded to the human shape.

A world of interest! A whole shelf with an array of hats, which made me long to try for fun and fit: top hats, bowlers, a fez. Everywhere — photos, portraits, pen drawings. . . Maps, models, medical pictures. . . Quiet landscapes, full-masted ships beating downwind. . . Butterflies. . . Lovely soft-eyed babies and children. A house so wonderfully warm, enticingly inviting, somehow made vital, alive, welcoming! A haven. . . a *home!* I felt enveloped by it and knew someone aware lived here, enthusiastic, at peace, free!

Then Dr David's study: a quietness I could feel, pleasing, tasteful. A complete wall of books. A music stand accompanied by its cello, polished to a rich sheen. A striking black marble fireplace. Portraits of loved ones. These my eyes took in, my mind experienced.

And there standing beside his austere desk was the doctor, very tall, startlingly fair, unassumingly friendly, like a comfy, big overgrown schoolboy; yet, as I was to learn, far more than that: a deeply compassionate human being.

He'd already read a brief account of my life, so shared some of his experiences and explained his method of helping me. I knew it was all right; I could trust this man. We moved to begin my therapy. Another surprise: this room was completely covered with mattresses, each spread with coloured quilts. Heaped about were dozens of cushions of every size: stripes and florals, some with intricate patchwork, others quite plain. They served me well over the next three weeks, those cushions, for I threw them and wrestled with them, jumped on them, wept into them and even hugged them. How I grew to love that room, but at first I was very nervous.

'Just settle yourself comfortably, Cathy Ann,' Dr David said as he sat, quietly, cross-legged beside me, 'and breathe deeply. First, I'll ask the Holy Spirit to show us what is necessary for your healing. Now I want you to find any place you are hurting and intensify it.'

Intensify it! I wanted to shout with joy and gratitude, for here was further evidence of God's steady progression in my life. Intensify it! This was how I had been working over these last two years; not actually physically intensifying my emotional pain, but asking God to amplify it and to show me what had caused my emotional suffering and, more importantly, to show me the decisions I had made, the adapting my mind had done for me and the effects these were having on my life, trying all the time not to escape.

I'm not really very brave, so asking God to do this is always hard for me, but I had made the discovery that to continue to try to escape from my pain no longer worked for me. I had tried many ways to hide from my internal suffering. They included not acknowledging, even to myself, that I hurt. I had tried to ignore my suffering, or fill my mind with many thoughts and activities. I call this way of coping just plain 'filler'. It appears to be a great way of escaping and not facing something which ought to be faced, yet utterly fails to heal.

I had taken medication in the belief this might ease my pain. It stopped me, not the pain. I had even tried hoping it would all go away if I pretended it wasn't there: a vain hope. I had thought of more drastic measures when I was really low and sadly sometimes I had just given up, becoming completely controlled by my own pain. But none of these ways had produced any healing for me.

I had learnt that I must face my pain and suffering. To do this I had to see clearly the ways I use to escape facing my pain and then, with God's help, make a decision and try not to apply these methods of evading my suffering again. I do not find this facing my pain an easy way to live, yet for me it produces a healing that not facing my emotional pain fails to give.

Now – how wonderful! – here was this highly qualified doctor telling me to do, physically, exactly what I had discovered really worked for me emotionally. Intensify my pain. Face it, experience it, bear it, even work on it.

This was the reassurance I needed in my life. I must enter into it as deeply as possible.

We worked steadily together for nearly three weeks, making worthwhile and life-changing discoveries, until there were only four more sessions to go.

'I don't feel right about pouring all my horrors on you as I've been doing,' I told David.

'I let it go straight to God,' he assured me. 'I am part of the church: together we share your suffering.'

His assurance freed me to continue. I began to weep quietly. After a while I became aware of my jaw working, as it were, of its own volition. I felt it with my hands. It was hard and wide open as though to explode out the screams emanating from the depths of my fear. Not a sound! Here was that heart-breaking, silent cry of my terrorised childhood. Soon I began to get in touch with a feeling of being restricted. Where? Around the ankles, around my chest and back. David's voice: 'Intensify this feeling.'

I tightened every muscle, every tendon, crunched up every bone and ached all over. David's voice came again: 'Find the picture; look at the picture. What do you see? What was the original happening in which you were bound, in your person or in your emotions? What were you bound with? Ropes? Chains? Thonging?'

I looked. I saw a leather belt. I felt so tied up, so tight. Immediately I was back there, just a little toddler. . .

Big tears are rolling down my cheeks. The edge is hard and uncomfortable and I'm slipping; my backbone is scraping as I slide down. Rounded knees are pushing up into my face and I'm sore where my legs are pushed tight on to the rim of the pottie.

I'm all hunched up and it hurts. I just can't get up and walk away either, because Mummy and Daddy have tied that long old leather belt around my ankles. It's the belt Daddy uses to beat us with, the one with the buckle. They've pulled it right round the pottie with my arms jammed right down each side. Little fingers and feet are getting funny and all numb where they are pushed on to the cold red tiles on the bathroom floor.

'Please let me off, Mummy!'

Daddy comes in laughing and pointing his finger, trying to peer under my legs. What does he want to see?

I feel awful sitting here strapped to this pottie and I'm sort of caught under the rim of the bath, too. I can see its feet like big pussy cat's feet, made of hard stuff, and the bath just sits on them where it curves under. If I wriggle a bit I can get out from under its rim. Oh no! The pottie's made a scratchy noise on the floor. That means Mummy or Daddy will come in again now and want to know if I've done anything. I can't; I don't even want to. They will look at me all strange again, too, and tighten up Daddy's belt; it hurts so much already.

Daddy looking at me is like when I'm older, about six or seven, and down sitting on the old tin toilet in the little lavatory in the garden. Suddenly Daddy's head pokes under the big space at the bottom of the door and he looks up at me.

'What do you keep looking at, Daddy? I'm just your little Annie. My feet don't even touch the floor. Why do you peep under the lavvy door, Daddy? I wish you would go away and not do that. You look strange and not very nice upside down and sticky-beaking like that. Go away, Daddy – go away!'

He is very proper, my daddy. No-one must go anywhere near the toilet when he's there and it must never ever be mentioned. I never do! When I go to the lav I'm really frightened of making a noise in case someone hears. Then they'll know I'm there and will put their head under the door and look up at me – I think. No-one ever does, though; only Daddy.

'You can come out now, Cathy Ann.' David's voice, as though from a great distance, broke through to me. We sat quietly and shared, even laughed. 'It's all part of the healing,' David told me. 'For the pain you come to know is the pain you can let go.'

These are the steps David has explained to me: *first*, acknowledge your pain; *second*, intensify it – this is frequently followed by discovering and facing what caused it; *third*, let go and release, sometimes accompanied by laughter. These three steps together began the healing process. They enabled me to face many problems, especially the problems which had come from my parents' toilet training.

What an effect this has had on my life. It was not helped by that big dose of senna tea Father made us drink every Saturday, or after any party we might occasionally attend. The cleansing process it was supposed to produce never left me in any doubt of its efficacy and the taste was revolting. Clare and I have never been able to enjoy a real 'cuppa' all our lives.

The worst effects, though, were not physical but emotional. The feelings of restriction, having always to be so very proper; the constraints placed on just having fun, on feeling free to move and even sit, in a relaxed manner; the fear of doing the wrong thing or not doing the right thing: these always haunted me. Expecting punishment for not producing the required results; never seeming to be able to please others; afraid of not pleasing God; being constantly controlled by an unseen yet absolutely real, for me, restriction: these were some of the effects which now must be faced.

Discovering how, as a child, I had been physically bound revealed how the adult equally was invisibly yet effectively restrained, unable to escape. Now, making my own decisions to move further into my suffering, I know that the very act of being willing to go deeper into suffering and face it for what it is has enabled me to move on through it and out of that particular pain into freedom on the other side.

After David had left the 'cushion room', I did some somersaults; a room full of cushions is one of the few safe places for a lady in her fifties to attempt such outlandish gymnastics. I wasn't much good. But it was tremendous fun!

Journey through pain

Pain and suffering hang low around me,
secretly concealed by light talk,
much activity, laughter.
Ever present yet not always physical
pain permeates my life,
trying to stifle joy and peace.
Is 'flight' the answer,
or to ignore the internal anguish?
My desire is to shun pain,
never more to know suffering.
                To escape!

Yet to live is to suffer the lot of each one.
Pain's guises are many,
its effects far-reaching.
For rejection, despair, hatred,
frustration and separation,
the heartbreaking endurance of illness,
loneliness and death can invade us.
Each decision can change us,
make time irretrievable,
love never shared.
                Loss inescapable!

When pain springs forth to stab our souls,
what does it teach us
with its piercing thrust?
To waste it or use it?
To try to escape it?
As though we could wrench suffering from our lives,
choosing instead self-gratification
by setting our minds rigidly towards pleasure,
seeking release from reality,
anything which offers a way out of pain.
          An apparent escape!

Could I face pain?
Doggedly follow each path it leads me,
grapple with its subtle maze.
At last striving not to escape,
but to enter its depths, meet its malice,
involve my mind in it. Intensify it!
Have I the courage to grasp pain's hurt,
embrace the fullness of its unleashed fury?
Face its torment, acknowledge its degradation,
struggle on through it?
          No escape in this?

An amazing contradiction: by facing my pain
I have come forth victorious –
albeit a bedraggled victor, mud-spattered and torn.
Still I am jubilant,
for I confronted my pain,
determined yet fearful.
Then in the calm of completion
I discover a companion,
he who has not left my side for a moment.
The suffering Christ.
Now triumphant!

9

The unutterable loneliness

VIOLATED. . . yes. . . but somehow unprofaned!

This was how I spent my childhood, as though a part of me existed in some special way, untouched by the abuses I suffered. I was able to remain loyal to myself, maintain my own identity and within my spirit preserve my integrity.

Then I entered secondary school. What a singular time for me: so much to learn, a whole new world opening up to my eager questing mind. All there for me to take, to use, to develop – yes, to enjoy. The wonder of my own potential, my worth as a human person were blossoming into adulthood with great vitality and enthusiasm.

The first eight or nine months fulfilled my keenest expectations. My mind operated with quick precision, soaring ahead to unexplored discoveries. My body moved and functioned with ease and grace, my soul floated in warmth and well-being. The horrors of my childhood were concealed far from my conscious mind behind their wall.

One day after school as I sat in the sunshine on the front lawn of a schoolfriend's house, she whispered to me about an amazing discovery she had made: the full details about the sexual act and other facts about becoming a woman. Although I had repressed from my conscious mind the experiences I had endured at my father's hands, this information about human sexual activity chilled me to the bone and I did not understand why.

A few days later, my father arrived home from work in one of his silent, seething rages. One of his plans had been thwarted. I recall his bitterness, his vindictiveness: he would get someone for this! My mother also saw the signs and, as she had done on previous occasions, set me up. Taking Clare she went out, leaving me alone at home that night to face that indescribable anger. My father made me stand beside him as he wrote several of his spiteful letters, then began his subtle manoeuvres to have his sexual needs met. Since hearing my schoolfriend's information, I knew some truths about this behaviour and, taking all my courage, I refused to be involved in this activity. He grabbed me. I beat on his chest, begging him not to touch me, sobbing. . .

'You mustn't, never again. It's wrong. I'm growing up. You must leave me alone!'

His anger exploded. He knocked me to the floor, kicking and dragging me through the house, yelling at me. 'How dare you defy me! You're bad through and through! You're evil! Not fit for decent people to associate with. And so proud. I'll teach you to defy me! I'll break you, you proud conceited bitch. You'll never defy anyone again, ever!'

He kicked me down our four back steps and stood glaring down at me. 'You filthy, dirty scum!' he snarled. 'You evil vulgar creature. You need me to really lay in the boot. I'll teach you to cross me!'

I lay there powerless as he loomed over me, in my terrified imagination looking like a vulture ready to swoop on me with its vicious claws. For one moment the scene was seared into my mind, then abruptly he let out a yell and jumped, just grazing me as he landed and, grabbing me by the hair and shoulder, dragged me into an enclosed verandah. He opened his huge hand and slapped me hard across the face. Then, catching me as I staggered, he clawed with his thick, tough nails right down my cheek. Still clutching me, he swung me around the room by the arms and, suddenly raising his foot, kicked me full in the stomach. I crumpled and sank to the floor.

'Please Daddy, don't, no more!' Clinging to his legs, I was begging, pleading. 'I love you, Daddy! I'm bad. . . all bad. I'm sorry, I'm sorry. . . I won't do anything wrong again. Don't hit me any more.'

He clenched his fist and crashed it down on top of my head. I think I fainted, for the next thing I remember was being in my bed with his huge form full length over me trying to rape me. I began to moan, with the sound rising to a shriek. He stopped, as though he saw he had gone too far, and swore violently. In the dim light from the hall I saw him move rapidly and snatch a pillow from Clare's bed.

Next moment he was forcing it down over my face.

'I must try and hold it off, must fight.' I'm gasping for breath, fighting to stop my dad trying to smother me, soundlessly screaming within myself: 'Don't give up. Oh God! Break his arm, do something! Help!'

I can hear someone opening the front door. Mummy? Clare? Nothing!

Then softly through the mists I hear sobbing. It's Clare, kneeling beside my bed, holding my hand, weeping. Clare is here. Clare will stay with me. . .

Much later I hear Mummy's voice, thick and angry. 'Leave her alone, Clare. Go to bed this instant. She's been very wicked while I've been out and you'll get worse if you don't do as you're told. Now go!'

Next day when my mother saw me, clawed and battered, she let out a raucous laugh and spat in my face. 'It's all your own fault. You're no good and deserve any punishment you get,' she derided me. But to our family doctor, whom they eventually had to call because I was so ill, they said: 'Oh, poor Ann. She fell down the back stairs. . . We'll look after her. Poor Annie, always so clumsy.'

For nearly two months I was unable to go to school and barely left the house. My mother went out often during that time, leaving me so desperately alone, more alone than anyone could possibly have comprehended. For, although my father had attacked me before, this time was different; he had broken my soul, completely disrespected my integrity, smashed that spirit which had lived secretly within me, keeping alive someone untouched and innocent within that poor little abused body. She was gone!

Oh, the unutterable loneliness, the isolation and devastation, that awful hopeless emptiness. I felt as if I was the shell of a person degraded, despised, finished. . . but must live on, a cowering coward, hating myself, sick with guilt, longing to die, pretending that within me that vivacious, enthusiastic person was still the same; but she was not. It seemed the child within me had died a terrible death.

It's a miracle to me that I was still alive at all. Why had my father stopped in his attempts to smother me? What had held his hand? I feel sure he could have made up some plausible story if I had died. Was it Clare's timely return from the neighbour where mother had left her which had obviously disconcerted him? I think here is a mystery which is part of all miracles: the timing of them. Had Clare returned minutes later it could have been too late. I remembered my silent scream to God to 'do something! Help!'

Despite this, within me rise up the queries, the doubts. For often as I have recited the Lord's Prayer the words 'deliver us from evil' have made me angry, because frequently I have felt that I was not delivered from evil, but plunged more deeply into it and left to struggle there alone, apparently with God unheeding and uncaring. But now as I relive the experience of that brutal beating and possible murder, a new thought stirs me: God *did* deliver me from evil. . . I am still alive. . . I am sane.

I am not suggesting that God sits in some 'ivory tower'

looking down upon all the suffering in this world and brushes it aside as though it is not evil and does not matter. For he, more than anyone, can see and comprehend how cruel and heartbreaking our suffering really is. Now, after all these years of doubts, I am coming to believe that he cares deeply and longs to draw us to himself, in some mysterious way using our pain in this process. He himself enters into our pain, giving his Son Jesus Christ to take our guilt and die in our place.

Believing that changed Rob's life and mine in our early twenties. Such joy burst upon me when I received God's forgiveness, love and acceptance – all special gifts from him for which my whole being had craved. Yet, just as my childhood had been snatched from me, over the years my experience of God slowly altered: a sense of separation from God began to permeate my being, causing me much sorrow and heart-searching. I had known God, been touched by his presence and found that hiding place for my lonely, guilt-laden soul. But again, I was searching for the answer to my question: 'Where are you, God?'

A gradual, insidious change had penetrated my relationship with God. I began to rely on friends who believed, on my past experiences of him, on doctrines and teachings. I struggled to maintain my closeness with God, using every means to keep my spiritual life going. But through it all I was not able to feel that I really trusted him. This last state was worse than the first.

Does this mean that Christianity is useless, or that God has failed? No. The years of feeling separated from God, though painful, have been used to deepen my understanding of how it can be for others who also have experienced this aloneness. Those years have enabled me to see that I am not self-sufficient, but need an awareness of God's presence constantly in my life.

Gradually I begin to comprehend that all through my own isolation God was there, weeping when I wept, hurting when

I hurt, and caring when I knew the degradation of being unloved and spat upon. He was with me in each experience, wrapping me in his love, easing me with his presence, firmly teaching me to trust him.

I am now able to see that holding in balance what I believe with what I feel enables me to know that all my life is part of his inexplicable purpose.

Paradox pardoned

Life is a paradox
balanced by opposites.
Sad when it's joyful
and free while constrained.
    Strength proved in weakness
    and courage in fear.
    Kindness knows cruelty
    and hope its despair.

Love weeps for hatred
and goodness for evil.
Success springs from failure
and feelings stir facts.
    Faith lives with doubts
    and trust knows rejection.
    Isolation seeks solace
    and pain lurks in pleasure.

Peace torn from discord
and sharing from selfishness.
Justice needs mercy
for living holds death.
    Who can explain that
    vast creativity
    released by our suffering
    or growth generated by pain?

We seek to hold all
in harmonious balance,
yet our good and our evil
strive to gain dominance.
    Desiring perfection
    we discover our faults.
    Then our best efforts fail
    to erase our own guilt.

*So we go our own way
in search of completeness,
while questioning God
to make sense of it all.
    But our ways are not his,
    for God seeks the contrite,
    not those content
    in their self-satisfaction.*

*It defies understanding –
love before power.
Only God has the answers;
he alone can deliver us.
    For when we acknowledge
    our need of forgiveness,
    Christ's death, that great paradox,
    has purchased our pardon.*

10

The parental bonds

WORDS HOLD SUCH POWER. They can deeply affect our lives, they can build or break us, motivate or stifle us. Words can fill us with love, encourage and strengthen us, enabling us to lead satisfying, fulfilling lives; or they can leave us broken and hurt, drained of our potential, our promise smothered and made useless by a thoughtless word or a cruel phrase.

How often have I longed to retrieve, somehow snatch from the air a word, a remark made lightly in jest or harshly in anger, or with subtle spite, yet cannot. . . Too late!

Or how often could I have spoken – should have spoken – just a word to express love, gratitude and affirmation to encourage another and yet I did not. . . I do not. . . For this it's not too late.

For me, words can be therapeutic. I find frequently, when I write them, this very activity eases my pain. Even at times pouring out my deepest feelings on some odd scrap of paper in some incongruous situation offers me solace. One day I wrote thirty pages in large, thick letters, emblazoning my hurt, my anger, across each clean white page, somehow purging my soul with the words 'I hate you!' – writing of my father, writing of God, writing of myself.

My father was very cruel with words. These often scarred us as severely as his physical cruelty. He used them to humiliate us and undermine our confidence, for we felt the lash of his bitter tongue and the sting of his sarcasm on many occasions.

Clare has a lovely voice and no small talent at the piano. When she sat down to practise, Father had his own special meanness. He would throw his head back and yowl, shouting, 'Listen to the cat's chorus!' Intimidated yet determined, Clare practised even harder, trying as always to find some humour in it.

Often through the hurt and heaviness, a shaft of humour has come to delight us both. I recounted to Clare another occasion when I told Father how he had hurt me and begged him not to. This aroused his anger and he turned on me, ordering me never to say anything as rude as that again; he did not want to hear such words. He explained that he needed to bring that lesson home clearly, so he pushed a pencil into my ear, threatening to press it right through.

As I told Clare about this memory, she was her usual calm self. She's very proper is my dear sister, but just occasionally the situation and her humour overcome her. 'Oh yes, I remember that,' she said. 'The bloody pencil in the ear trick!'

Some words were obligatory in our household, but very difficult for me to say at times. These were expected of me after my father had 'taught' me one of his cruel lessons, for after each I must say, 'May I leave now please, Daddy?' If by chance I omitted to add the other requirement, he would call me back and demand that I say 'Thankyou Daddy!', no matter what he had done to me, nor how badly I felt.

All these things affected me greatly and so must have affected my own children also. Just recently my eldest daughter, Sarah, told me some ways this had happened and gave me a few of the notes she had written in the form of letters to me about it: things she felt she couldn't say to me; feelings she had which hurt too much to express out loud; how she was endeavouring to cope with what was happening to me, because this was concerning her and the whole

family. No-one lives their lives without touching and in-
fluencing those around them. If one member of a family is
hurting, all are involved; each other member is in some way
part of that suffering. Though some may even pretend
indifference or not appear to be hurting, each expresses their
participation in their own way.

At her suggestion I am including several of these letters:

Dear Mum,
Well, it explains so much about our relationship, doesn't it?
Over the last few years, it's been stormy and hard for us both.
You know I told Brian [her husband] about your father
throwing fountain pens at you and beating you senseless and
he said that your father probably raped you as well. But you
never told me. It's true, isn't it?
Oh Mum, the pain is unbearable. All I can do is weep for
you. I can't even be with you. This despair is so overwhelming. Oh Mum, I can't even help you.
Gotta go. . . **Sarah**

> *Dear Sarah,*
> *Thanks for caring so much; it warms me. It really was so*
> *awful that I was unable to remember or face the fact of my*
> *violation myself for a long time. Love, Mum*

Dear Mum,
Please don't tell me any more, Mum! I can see such clear pictures of what you're saying and they come back to me and
haunt me.
I hurt all over; I've cried for days. I see this child torn and
broken and, worst of all, unloved and rejected. At one time
I thought it was me who was that child, but it was you all
along. But I've understood for so long your feelings of
having been rejected that I feel and know part of your pain.
I just can't see you this week. **Sarah**

Dear Mum,
Some things are making more sense. You know, I realise that
I must have picked up a lot of emotions from you. I told you
about feeling rejected and this overwhelming, all-pervading
fear. It's so strong that I've always had to be nice to
everyone, because if anyone was cranky with me I got really
scared. Especially in my relationships with men. And I
could never ask them anything in case they said no and then
I couldn't cope.
Please don't be sad. This is not bad. It's good for me to
know. Now I can change. **Sarah**

Dear Mum,
I hate him! I hate him! I hate him!
If he weren't dead I would go and kill him. I would stab him
and cut squares of flesh off and castrate him!
How can you say you don't hate him? I know he was your
father, but after what he did?
Oh, the unbearable pain.
All I can do is cry and try to wash the pain away. **Sarah**

> *Dear Sarah,*
> *Sometimes I hate him, too! I'm still pretty mixed up about*
> *them both, but so happy with you. I've found it helps to*
> *cry, even while it hurts. Love, Mum*

Mum,
You don't see, do you? You tell me this stuff and dump it on
me like a lorry load of rubbish and then expect me to cope.
You just pour it all over me like a stinking mire. Well, what
am I supposed to do with it? It's your emotional garbage, so
you deal with it; don't lay it on *me*. **Sarah**

> *Dear Sarah,*
> *I'm sorry, I was too involved with myself to see you were*
> *hurting. You seemed to be coping so well, treating me with*

professional calm and encouraging me to talk and share. I
failed to realise how deeply it was affecting you. You're
right, it is my emotional garbage. I'm still learning how to
handle it. It helped me very much to share it with you.
Love, Mum

Later, after a tearful phone call:

Dear Mum,
I know I shouldn't have told you off, but you wind yourself
up into these hyperventilating emotional whirlwinds and
they seem so totally destructive. Sure I believe in expressing
emotions, but not creating more and definitely not doing it
in a way that doesn't resolve anything. I know there are better ways of dealing with them. We'll pray together about it.
OK? Love, **Sarah**

Dear Mum,
Don't talk negative! I know that you can work through this
pain and hurt and all that happened in your childhood. I
know you can and I know that in time you will. Sure, there
is more to work through, but I know you can do it. You're
so strong, you've held yourself together for so long, you've
managed to rear three kids and look after so many houses.
You can do it and don't ever say you can't again. Love,
Sarah

> *Bless you, Sarah, for that very sound advice. I've never had*
> *that type of destructive reaction again since you explained*
> *it to me and you are right. God has shown me much better*
> *ways of coping. I can see now there is a type of crying*
> *through pain which is healing and also a type of crying*
> *which is self-indulgent.*
>
> *I know now that the 'healing' way of facing my childhood,*
> *though painful, is to work on it, alone or with Dr David or*
> *others, with God in control of the whole process; then for*

him to take me through it all, by getting me past the barrier of self-pity into the area where the emotion was originally repressed. God can then release it and I can begin to be healed. So thanks, darling, for your insight. Love, Mum.

Dear Mum,
Brian and I were talking about having children eventually. When I fall pregnant, can I spend lots of time with you, talking about babies and what to do? You know, that is something I'd really like to do with you!
Would you look after our kids, too, especially if I have to go back to work? Love you, **Sarah**

Dear Sarah,
What a wonderful thought. I'd be absolutely delighted. Thanks. Love, Mum.

Dear Mum,
I know you're only trying to be assertive, but Mum, you've gone overboard. Please don't be so damned aggressive. Honestly Mum, it's too much. Love you, **Sarah**

Dear Sarah,
Hopefully I'll reach a balance soon. It sure would be easier for all of us! Love, Mum.

Dear Mum,
I know we don't spend a lot of time together and I'm sorry that I don't read your work, but sometimes it's all too intense and I just can't cope. I'm not so angry or so hurt, but when we talk or when I read your poetry and stuff, it makes me weep. I guess I've still got a lot to work through.
But I'm proud to be your daughter and proud that you've fought so hard to survive. Mum, I really have a great deal of respect for you. I'm glad we can be friends. Your ever loving daughter, **Sarah**

Thanks, Sarah, I really appreciate all you've said and done. I know even more clearly now how you have all suffered because of what happened to me and it makes me hopping mad and really upset. But surely God can even use all that and not waste it – I'm asking him to anyway! Thanks, love, your Mum

*   *   *

These letters make it apparent that my unresolved problems had repercussions on my children. One of these problems which plagued my life and likewise carried over on to my children was the inconsistencies and double messages I experienced from my parents. I can see the harm the contradictions from my childhood have caused, for often I was loved yet hated, accepted yet rejected, caressed yet beaten, and I was hopelessly torn between those opposites.

Also the contrasts in my own nature have confused me, for I can be happy while sad, kind yet cruel, trusting yet fearful; within me there is my light and my dark side, the known and the hidden. At last I am able to admit these are all part of me, each striving for dominance at different times and occasions. And I am learning that when they are acknowledged by me and given to God, then I can accept them. I need no longer be afraid of them. I need not feel guilty about them, except if I choose to use them wrongly. I need no longer deride myself because of my ambivalence, for all these opposites make up the whole me.

This allows me to acknowledge that the conflicts within myself have caused confusion for Sarah, Grace and Bart. Dr David told me I used to present two distinct messages to the family. One message appeared to say: 'I am in pain, I am fearful, I do not trust anyone or God. I am angry and worthless. I don't think anyone loves me and, though I love others, I can't seem to do it properly. I am rejected and sometimes rejecting. I am confused and need help. Please help me!'

In contrast, the other message I was sending said: 'I can cope. I love you, but I don't believe you love me. I am religious, so I trust God and others and I shouldn't feel anger. I don't have any reason to feel worthless, so I don't really feel that way. Look and see for yourselves. I am pleasant and not confused – I don't need help. So back off!'

I was saying: 'Please understand these messages, even if I don't.' Yet they were totally contradictory messages! I can see how this could utterly confuse my children, especially when they were young, for they would not know how to react to me.

There are still other areas of my life I'd like changed and also in the children's lives. But who am I to say if and how the family need changing? For they are their own people. It's one of the special things I've always prayed for each of them: that they would become individuals in their own right and use their God-given potential.

One day when I muttered that I thought they were a bit too way out, Grace commented: 'Mum, you wanted us to be individuals. You always told us that. Well, what are you complaining about? Look at us. We definitely are all individuals!' Rob and I could only completely agree. We had wanted this for them, most particularly, so they could grow and develop as the unique persons they are. Such a different attitude to my parents' expectations of me!

More words seemed to spring into my mind. Demanding words, binding words, words from my parents, words which seemed to ring through my childhood in many forms: 'Shut up!' 'Give up!' 'Pay up!'

'Shut up!', because nice little ladies are seen and not heard. 'Shut up!', because we do not discuss our business with a single soul in the family or outside of it.

'Give up!' Whatever is yours, my child, belongs to us. I need you now, because I am unhappy and need cheering up; I am angry and need someone to hit; I have a sexual urge and you must meet it; I want to play a sadistic trick upon someone and you'll do. You belong to us!

'Pay up!' You must do this for Mummy and Daddy. We brought you into this world and have a right to anything from you. You owe us!

Lately I have been reading the Lord's Prayer, using a different translation by K.S. Wuest. Instead of the well-known 'Forgive us our sins as we forgive those who sin against us', Wuest states: 'Forgive us the moral obligations we owe even, as for us, we have forgiven those morally obligated to us.'

The moral obligations we owe. These words hit me like a sledge-hammer, for they placed me in a position of indebtedness. Not just the plural 'we owe', but 'I owe' as an individual. I *owed* my parents. I was morally obligated to them. 'You owe us,' they often said. I feel it even now that I am bound to them. If I owe something, it needs to be paid – and, in their case, frequently repaid and paid again.

Looking back, this was all too much for me, especially as a small child. It was another weight to place upon fragile, already heavily laden shoulders – as though I owed my parents something because I was indebted to them, so they could do whatever they wanted. It overshadowed my very existence.

Suddenly it is as though I am again that child, involved totally in their requirements, under their control, and I know to my horror that I am insurmountably in debt, hopelessly in arrears with a debt which cannot ever be repaid, a debt which cripples my life, strangles my development, stifles my individuality and deadens my creativity. From this debt they can ceaselessly extract exorbitant repayments and remorselessly add to it every action of mine, be it good or bad. I am totally indebted to them – not out of love, but because they demanded it. It is a debt which binds me to them even more tightly than the leather belt by which they strapped me to objects as a child.

This great sense of liability, which seems unpayable, unbreakable and irremovable, can be discharged. Not paid, not forgotten, not removed nor ignored, not broken, but forgiven!

Yes, forgiven, because the price of it – too high for me to pay, too expensive for my most sincere endeavours to discharge – has been paid entirely by God's Son. I cannot understand nor fathom the complexities of it, but I know this payment is fully satisfactory to God. My debt to my parents is paid in full. No longer need I be bound by it.

With this setting free from my own debt comes another discovery. Have I laid upon my own children this sense of indebtedness to me? Have I placed them under bondage to me, just as I was under bondage to my parents? Do they strive for their freedom? They are, in reality, not indebted to Rob and me yet, because we all love each other, there is a bond of caring, of sharing. But not the cruel confining I had from my parents.

My desire is that the obligations between us will only be the bonds of love and mutual forgiveness.

Yet because my parents were not trustworthy, I've never felt sure I could trust others. I did not believe others could love me. In my mind I knew Rob, Sarah, Grace and Bart did love me, but in my emotions I was unable to grasp this. Now as my mind and emotions, the facts and my feelings, are coming together, I'm ready to take the risk and believe I am worth loving. I am delighting in the love and acceptance of my family and the new openness this brings.

Also it thrills me to say I am learning to trust my fellow humans more fully without fear of them. It is not because they never fail but, in spite of their imperfections, knowing they struggle, they hurt and feel fear as I do and they, too, long to be loved. And I choose to take the risk and trust and love these fallible people and be loved in return.

As I admit I am loved and loving, and sometimes I am hated and hating, I realise my life will not fall apart and disintegrate because I hold opposing views, do contrary things and learn new and differing opinions. These are all part of being human and humans have worth. I know this because my family and friends have shown me that people care about others, even those unknown to them. People are of value to others, therefore I, too, am of value and worth, for I am a person.

I believe I will always feel differently from others because of my background, but that hidden self-hatred which had previously undermined my life only occasionally haunts me now. So I can begin to be at ease about who I am, I can relax and have fun, I can accept the decisions I make and not be overwhelmed by uncertainties, I can take responsibility for what I do with my life and not be driven by fear.

I can move on to the steps to my recovery. I no longer need to live my life as a victim of the past.

PART TWO:

ROAD MAP FOR SURVIVORS

11

Our common
hopeful place

BREAKING THROUGH the barrier of my terrible childhood is moving my life along a new road and giving me clearer insights into the effects of child abuse. I needed to find a way to cope for I was constantly confronted by a question which demanded an answer, a question which still plagues many victims: *Will I ever recover from this hell I live in*?

Adults who were abused as children fling that question at me in conferences, nervously ask it in groups or, between sobs, whisper it in private. I know what hell they mean. I've been there, too! I don't just mean the hell of remembering the abuse from my childhood. The cruel bite of memories fades, physical pain eases, but the emotional damage remains.

That damage from my abuse had torn to shreds any personal sense of worth in me and filled me with self-hatred, fears, guilt, anger and deep depression. These and worse are part of the hell most abused persons live and struggle with, albeit with varying problems and degrees of difficulty. Before I remembered my hidden childhood I was haunted by these soul-destroying evaluations of myself; programmed to believe I was worthless and unlovable. Yet I could not discern the reason.

Now I know! My parents' cruelty caused my inner heartache and their failure to love and nurture me robbed me of the feelings of acceptance essential for my emotional well-being.

When my first repressed memories began erupting during counselling, I assumed I had a choice. I could stop – or I could go on and unlock the door of my past. But I could not stop! I knew facts I had not consciously known before and could never again unknow. It was impossible to stay in that limbo of knowing so little, yet just too much! Nor could I return to my former state. The effort required to maintain the pretence that I was loved and acceptable had become intolerable to me. The intense unhappiness of my internal life, spreading like an emotional cancer through my whole being, was leading me to total collapse. In fear and desperation I went on, deciding I'd face anything, fight like blazes and somehow get through, or – so I believed – die in the attempt.

I have gone on and faced the scenes of terror, hatred and cruelty which I lived through as a child, but apparently locked away as soon as they happened, for I could not deal with them then, nor the emotions they produced.

The debasing effects of that abuse have not only marred the childhood of most victims; their devastating emotional consequences have permeated – even contaminated – the teenage years and their long-term ongoing repercussions have had a crippling influence on the lives of too many adults.

After the memories of my parents' abuse came flooding back into my conscious awareness, my only knowledge of child abuse was confined to what had happened to my sister, Clare and myself. As I began to tell my story, to my distress and amazement I discovered there were more victims than I could possibly have imagined.

Were you abused as a child? The horror of being a victim! Who but you knows the effects of such a trauma on your life and what price the cost of surviving carries! Who can comprehend the devastation which occurs at the most formative stage of development in the life of the child victim of abuse? Our lives were changed, twisted into another direction, unable to follow what would have been their natural course. Usually we are left with deep hurts, many still buried; secrets too painful, too embarrassing to share; residual problems controlling us, affecting our day-to-day living and relationships. Because of the immense effort it takes many victims to survive, from now on I will call us 'survivors'.

We can never alter the events of our personal history. This being so, what can be done about the effects of such a childhood on our lives? What can we learn? How can we grow? What can we become in spite of, or even because of, the rejection and pain we lived through? An option that worked for me was stepping out with God.

If my story had stopped at the discovery of my abuse, with its debilitating effects still undermining my life; if I had continued with my hostility to God because I was unable to reconcile my beliefs in a loving, caring heavenly Father with the sense of desertion by him I felt as a child being abused; then I would have been without hope. Broken! Finished! But I am coming to grips with what seemed an intolerable situation.

Looking back, I realise that even in my darkest moments, a method of action was gradually emerging from the seeming chaos within to propel me towards recovery. Though I did not clearly recognise I was using them at the time, a set of steps were beginning to take shape to enable me to climb out of the pit of my suffering.

The understanding counselling I was receiving was only for one hour a week and I desperately needed help *twenty-four* hours a day. Mostly I was struggling alone and my own resources were inadequate to relieve my misery. Admitting that I could not solve my problems without a method which was available full-time gave me the impetus to persevere with the steps. They began to unblock the situation within me and redirect my mind and energies towards working with God, not pulling against him.

A gradual change in the whole direction and purpose of my life released me to become more aware that around me victims were endeavouring to cope in dreadful isolation. Suddenly the suffering of other survivors burst upon me in torrents, stirring me with pain, despair, compassion and an awesome rage. Something had to be done!

I was thankful and impressed to learn of the efforts of thousands of people who are dedicated to caring and working with children being abused now. But I was not meeting children in crisis: I was being confronted by teenagers and adults who are suffering at this very moment from *past* abuse. Its insidious effects are still tormenting their lives. The more fortunate ones, like myself, are receiving guidance with compassion and wisdom from understanding supporters who deserve our heartfelt gratitude.

Those of us who are receiving assistance, and sadly the many who are not, are searching for release, longing to escape. Escape I discovered was no answer! Yet there was a way through which was beginning to work for me. While my own need was the impetus, the needs of other survivors compelled me to strive to formulate more clearly the steps to give us a plan to follow in order to bring hope and recovery which can continue every day.

Using the steps began to revolutionise my life, allowing me to be honest with God about who I am, what I think and how I feel. They broke through barriers in me, giving God access to become the driving force in my recovery. I was able to face my childhood, to slowly break its suffocating control over my life and even come to grips with my hostility to God and people. Further, these steps were giving me and other victims *hope*.

The knowledge that there is hope is desperately needed by most survivors. Hope can start us going on our journey towards recovery. It gives us the courage to begin, then something to hold onto as we cautiously move forward.

My hope is steadily becoming based in God, but I must admit I am often in two minds about him. Though I believe God works in me, there are times when I throw up huge road-blocks, stating bluntly: 'Private property! Keep out!' This internal opposition heightens my pain and deepens the sense of my separation. Yet out of the realisation of the hopelessness of my ambivalence towards God and the inner pain and turmoil from the abuse I sustained as a child has begun to evolve a hope I want to offer you. For me, it's a different type of hope. I have found it especially relevant for hurting people and that's what I want to put before you – a workable hope.

These days the media bombards us with quick and easy ways to get things done and deal with living. The reality is that recovery is rarely either quick or easy for those of us who have been abused. We will need to move slowly and often painfully and have the courage to persevere, because the way out of our problems is usually a long, hard road, yet worth all the effort for both survivors and supporters.

I had just spoken to adults abused as children and their counsellors when a doctor I knew, holding herself very erect yet looking incredibly tired, came towards me. She had a demanding job in charge of a crisis centre for victims of incest in one of Australia's cities.

'I'm finding it hard to carry on,' she confided. 'There are so many victims! I drive around the city and as I pass house after house I find myself asking: "Is there a child being abused in there? Does an adult who was abused live there?" I'm doing my utmost to help them, but not with much hope for their recovery.'

For a moment or two she paused, then suddenly, with what seemed a sigh of relief, she took me by the shoulders, shook me vigorously and said: 'I've been watching you. I've listened to what you've said. You're coping. I can see your life is going somewhere: it's obvious you're recovering. Do you know, can you even guess what that means? People who've been abused can learn to live more effectively. It's worth keeping on. You've given me hope!'

Yes, I have hope – in God, myself and the steps. I am finding in all three potential for growth and change. I am learning there are alternative ways of seeing myself, of living, of transforming the scars which come from abuse to constructive uses. Gradually I am discovering a new perspective, with my failures becoming doors to achievements, forgiving is replacing condemning, hope is evolving from hopelessness. I am facing myself and my problems rather than fleeing from them. There is a growing realisation in me that even those times when I am down can become areas for learning and growing. I do not have to stay in that place of despair which is so common to those of us who have been victims.

That's a great encouragement! But if I am honest, I know I will fail again. I will want to escape from myself, leave my inner pain. I'm amazed how quickly and easily I can sink back into hopelessness. If I do I can start again, knowing that my recovery is ongoing and the intensity of my trauma will gradually ease. It's a process, a movement forward then backwards, then forward again. For me that's a hope worth having.

'Well,' a friend – endeavouring to be positive – informed me, 'my usual expectations of hope are that we will get what we want, without too much waiting, of course, and that we will always be in an "on top situation". Naturally we will be happy, at least most of the time. And being down or depressed I perceive as failure.'

I replied, also being very positive, 'My expectations of hope are that being down does not have to mean "hopeless". 'I can get up and press on. What makes it worth moving forward is that I can know that where I am going now is different from where I've been and it's ultimately better, less frightening, though maybe more exacting, even painful at times.'

'That's a different approach for sure,' my friend put in.

'My hope does *not* mean that everything in my life will be all right from now on,' I continued. 'I don't expect that God will always smooth my way, nor suddenly totally cure me, though sometimes this happens. I anticipate, because of how life is, that there will always be problems, highs and lows. At times I catch glimpses of a unified me occurring in what had been my hurting, fragmented self. This gives me confidence to press on.'

We humans are complex creatures and part of our complexity stems from our ability to function on several different levels at the same time. As we relate to others, what we feel inwardly may not always be discernible to them. These levels are frequently more extreme in those who have been abused as children, accentuating our inner despair. Externally we can be presenting one type of person who is relating fairly normally, while internally we may be plagued by feelings of worthlessness, depression, debilitating fears and the awful dread of going insane.

I remember years ago asking a friend how it was that he and other people coped so well when they felt so awful inside. There was a strange silence while he contemplated me. 'What do you mean? People don't feel awful inside,' he said.

'I know someone who does,' I stated. 'Me! I feel awful inside.'

That brave young man married me!

Because my abuse was so completely repressed, I did not associate my problems in the present with childhood traumas. I did not know why I felt such distress or why I was having such trouble coping. I could not comprehend its cause. This added to my anguish. That's the story of so many survivors.

While it seems that some survivors, whether they know

the cause of their troubles or not, cope well, some do not do so well and, sadly, some cannot keep going. The burden for them becomes so heavy they give up. They sink into illness, their minds might shatter or, worse, they kill themselves, perhaps without connecting a possible source of their inner torment with brutal childhood abuse. But still they, as we, are responsible for the decisions we make. Despair, a dark companion for many survivors, is highlighted because often no-one else, not even in our own family, felt able to admit that anything as horrific as abuse was happening.

We used to think of abuse as being the callous act of a stranger, but now we know a more degrading truth: frequently offenders are known, often even trusted, by the child, and at least eighty per cent of perpetrators are a close male relative: a father, step-father, brother, grandfather, uncle, cousin, close family friend, neighbour. No wonder trust for survivors is severely curtailed or even destroyed! Especially is this true now with the acknowledgement that some women, too, molest children. Can you begin to comprehend the fear, the anguish in never having a place where you are safe, not even your own home?

To add to our difficulties, so many of us were threatened by our abuser with dire consequences if we failed to keep our dreadful secret even from an early age. 'I will kill you, like I killed your dog.' Or, 'Your whole family will suffer if you tell and it will be all your fault.' What a responsibility for a frightened child to bear alone! What a terrible secret to have to keep, especially as so much of society appears to be oblivious to the lives being shattered daily in its midst.

The problems of victims are not helped by society's method of coping with abuse: *denial*. It is important, therefore, to recognise the facts: abuse occurs across the whole spectrum of society. It is present in every social class, religious or racial group, although some of these factors may inhibit the incidence of abuse.

What an overwhelming thought that very likely someone

you will see today was neglected, to the point of ill-treatment as a child, or emotionally, physically or sexually abused before the age of eighteen. The NSW Department of Education stated in the *Sydney Morning Herald* of 19 June 1987 that thirty per cent of girls and ten per cent of boys had unwanted sexual contact by this age. Mr Les Harrison, a clinical psychologist, is reported in the same paper on 23 April 1990 as telling a child protection conference at Macquarie University, NSW, that a recent Australian study had concluded that '. . . one in four girls and one in ten boys would be victims of sexual abuse by the age of eighteen.'

'Even if the numbers are only ten per cent of what is feared. . . that is scandalous!' stated Professor Kim Oates, President of the International Society for the Prevention of Child Abuse and Neglect.

Most victims of sexual molestation were, and still are, girls, but now more men are admitting to having been abused physically and sexually as children.

Tom, who had just told me his story of sexual abuse as a child, drew in a long breath then let it out in a soft, slow whistle: 'I've told someone at last! What a relief! I'm a psychologist. I'm over forty. Can you believe it – I've never told anyone that story before?'

All society suffers and is paying a terrible price for the neglect of those who are still suffering the consequences of their abuse. This adds up to untold thousands of children, teenagers and adults.

We who are survivors, our families, our relatives, friends, medical advisers, counsellors, church leaders and members, the wider society and the news media, need to accept the truth that the repercussions of abuse do have injurious consequences in our world. We can admit it happened to us. Our families and others need to admit it happens. But let's not be tricked into stopping there. Let's go on and acknowledge we all have been and still are being affected by this insidious evil and incalculable suffering.

We need to love, support and try to understand each other. Denial will not make abuse go away! Recognition and acknowledgement by society, on the other hand, will provide a more supportive environment for victims to move from their place of despair and begin to grasp the hope of recovery. This can enable them to break the many hurtful effects which have flowed through to their families and others in society from their suffering. These actions become significant factors in the prevention of more child abuse.

12

Our common
hurting place

IF ONLY! I've wondered that many times. If only I hadn't been treated that way as a child, what type of person would I be? How differently would I have coped if I'd been brought up in a happy home? The undeniable fact is the events of my childhood cannot be altered. Survivors need to accept this.

But must we also accept the consequences of our abuse as unalterable and continue to be plagued by their trauma? What can be done to lead us to a better existence so we can develop our innate capacities? For this development was interrupted, even redirected for too many survivors, undermining our ability to rise above the constraints of our abuse. Does this make us different from non-abused persons? If so, what is different about the way we survivors function?

At a dinner for caring people involved in working with abused teenagers, Marcie, a delightful sixteen-year-old, had been speaking about her own childhood abuse and what its heartbreaking effects had done to her view of herself. As she threaded her way between the tables towards me, a barrage of emotions hit me: pleasure, then anger, sadness, pain, despair. Again, unanswerable questions!

'I've been wanting to meet you so much,' her words bubbled

over me. 'I've read your book *No Longer a Victim* and feel I've known you all my life. I wanted to write my story. I felt everyone should know what happened to me. You've told my suffering to the world. You've written how it was for me.' Very moved, I said, 'I was proud of you up there telling your story. You were brave to be so honest.' We sat and talked, enjoying being together, knowing we had something painful yet, even so, very special in common.

Then Marcie said, 'I want to ask you something. I need to know your answer to this. Someone keeps telling me I'm different to everyone else. I don't believe I'm different. What do you think?' It wasn't hard to explain to her about the hurting place we have in common which I believe most survivors come from. She knew it instinctively.

'I believe the majority of those who have been abused, especially from an early age, come from what I think of as our same hurting place. It's that insecure base we've tried to build our lives on. I call it our "different basic reference point of defective nurture". Abuse caused such a disruption in us that it produced ways of "seeing" ourselves which were not necessarily right. But now they have become our inner beliefs about ourselves, making us respond differently to the way others respond who haven't had the same trauma. Most of us who've been abused have a different foundation we've built our lives on.'

'That's it, that's it!' The sheer relief in her face was a joy. 'I *respond* differently because I was abused. I can accept that difference. I'm still a human being like everyone else.' We hugged each other with enthusiasm, being aware of the strong hidden bond which gave us a warm, shared oneness.

Letters and conversations with other survivors have shown the rapport between us. I've found most of us respond, act and react from a different place to those from happier backgrounds where they were not abused. Their reference points are so different that it's often hard for them to comprehend the effect abuse has had on survivors.

Mother Theresa of Calcutta has said: 'We all come into this world expecting to love and be loved.' I believe that for too many children, instead of being loved and nurtured which is our rightful heritage, our expectations of love were shattered. We were abused. This applies particularly to those ill-treated from their earliest moments. I have observed also that calculated or, worse, sadistic abuse can cause intensely demoralising damage, especially if perpetrated by parents or carers on a very young child. Even if in some cases there was no overt physical abuse, the wounds of emotional abuse can go very deep and cause much harm.

For those assaulted at an older age, it's as though an inaudible bomb had shattered some, or many, of their previously held reference points of nurture and love. For all who have been abused either as children or later in life, this makes our relating not the same and even more difficult to that of non-abused persons. When I share the concept of different reference points with other survivors, their faces light up. 'It's like that for us, too!' they enthusiastically tell me.

It is not only victims of child abuse, of course, who come from a different foundation. Those who are handicapped or with special problems also have this other dimension.

Only minutes after I'd finished speaking, a rather imposing lady planted herself squarely in front of me. 'I'm the house mum for eight abused teenagers,' she informed me. I had particularly noticed her in the audience, sitting slightly forward with what looked like a frown barely leaving her face, making me more nervous than usual.

'Never!' she exclaimed. 'Never before have I understood why most of those kids at home seem to act so contrary to how I expect them to. Not quite like other kids. At last you've explained why that is. They're coming from a different place to the rest of us, aren't they? I see now they've been acting normally for them. That's going to make a big difference to the way I treat them. I can hardly wait to get home and try it out. I love 'em, you know.'

Nearly every victim has been deflected from how they might have been by abuse. For some the change may have been insignificant; for a great many others it could have been quite profound. Either way, our lives were altered because we were used and misused by another person for their gratification, for their sadistic cruelty or in anger, but certainly not for our well-being. The sense of our own value was smashed by the denial of our right as children to be treated as special and unique human beings and receive the love, respect and care which was our expectation. Our individuality was not honoured, but was violated by others. But somehow we have courageously picked up the scattered pieces and gone on functioning and living, attempting to cope through our childhood, teen years and on through adult life.

The assumption that my parents would love me and want me had been smashed by their abuse. It's true that no-one has had perfect parenting because no-one has been the perfect parent. We have all been subject to the frailties of human errors and failure in the giving and receiving of proper nurture. Thank goodness children can cope with imperfection. It's normal; *abuse is not* – no matter how common! But my parents' abuse had distorted my original concepts of myself, leading me to believe that I was of no value and that therefore I deserved to be abused. It put into action within me a whole new set of inner beliefs about myself.

For many survivors our inner beliefs, brought on by the trauma-producing and life-changing effects of child abuse, can bind us within a rigid limiting emotional structure which can inhibit our relating to others and our enjoyment of life.

Often we've been told, 'That all happened years ago. Forget it, get on with living. It's over and done with now.'

'If only this were so!' was the heartfelt response from a full-time worker with adult victims of incest. I wonder if people would say 'Forget it !' to the victims of the Holocaust. I hope not, but maybe some would. There are always people who think that to ignore emotions will cause them to go away. Ignoring emotions represses them, driving them deep into our subconscious where they fester. Such a shattering experience as the Holocaust would have changed the lives of its victims for all time.

Some survivors have lived through a heartbreaking personal holocaust of their own, frequently without anyone to share their fearful burden. We, too, long to 'put it aside'. . . but cannot. Mostly the incident is over, but the trauma and its consequences can and do go on and on and the memory stays always, sometimes hidden even from the victim.

I have observed – and others have told me – that when a situation or problem arises in our lives, we humans unconsciously look back into our earliest experiences to our reference point of nurture and we draw upon the love and nurturing we did or did not receive then. The sense of our own value, whether high or low, arises from this. We then make our decisions based upon our inner beliefs about ourselves. These beliefs are re-activated, even though our environment and circumstances may change many times. Over the years I've often wished I could get away to somewhere, anywhere, if only I could just leave the wounded *me* behind. For I look back and see abuse, hopeless childhood nurture and myself responding from that place all too often.

I wonder, if nurture could be measured on a scale of one to ten, where the adequacy of our nurture would put us on such a graph? Perhaps those who have been greatly blessed by receiving loving, balanced nurture may even score an eight or nine out of ten, while others who have been the recipients of adequate nurture, may rate a six to seven. Some who have had the less-than-adequate nurture – neglect – may be a five, and those who have been the objects of abuse may range from as low as a one to a four. Obviously we who have been abused come from the lower end of this imaginary scale. This has helped me to understand the devastating effects of our background of abuse more clearly.

The house dad, husband of the mum caring for 'At Risk' teenagers, came up to speak to me. I'd seen him, too, as I'd talked. He had his head down. Had I put him to sleep I'd wondered? Noisily blowing his nose, he said, 'I understand better now how those kids we look after feel about themselves. Just lousy! I'm sorry I never saw it so clearly before. I've been crying through your whole talk.'

I know our families, friends, therapists – in fact all who give of time and pour forth love on hurting survivors – desire above all to encourage us to develop and grow and become fulfilled in our lives. So we need you to grasp that many of us who have been abused physically, emotionally and sexually are still responding from that hurting place which others cannot fully understand unless they have been there. So please do not expect us to respond like non-abused people, because this expectation will not help you to care for us, encourage or love us, nor is it a workable basis for appropriate therapy.

A survivor husband blithely told his wife, 'Wow, this responding from different reference points has really let me off the hook. I can act how I like now and blame it all on that concept. What a great excuse!'

You won't get away with that, my friend! It's not an escape route. It's meant to help us honestly face our problems and encourage us in the way we relate to one another.

But survivors have extra problems on top of the usual impediments to living and relating which are common to all humanity: we live with the consequences our childhood traumas have produced in us. Because of our abuse, most of us have become super-sensitive, wary, easily hurt, plus many other reactions which are more marked than for non-abused persons, though we probably don't always recognise these in ourselves.

Survivors have specific ways of coping which can be recognised as coming from our particular background. Some

people speak of these as symptoms; to me they are identify-
ing traits. I call them *indicators*.

You'll notice that many people have some of these indicators; none is unique to abused persons. But if a person
has many of them, or they are very marked, they can show
the presence of an abused background which can help to
explain why survivors are functioning in a certain way. This
knowledge can also help determine what can be done for the
survivor who is presenting the problems.

With other survivors I have compiled a list of these
indicators. Don't be afraid if some of the list fits you. A
friend read it and threw up her arms in despair. 'I have
nearly all of those indicators,' she wailed.

I truly sympathised. That's quite a shock. What she
hadn't realised was that they are part of the imperfections of
being human. Most of us have some or many of them. I
tried to reassure her by suggesting: 'Now you've seen them
– don't panic! Here's your opportunity to do something
about them.'

Most survivors have indicators in varying degrees of
intensity, although frequently not recognised as a legacy from
their abused childhood. Indicators vary in strength and can
trouble survivors irrespective of their state of mind or external circumstances. They can point back to the different base
on which our lives have often been built and can point out
in the present the fact of abuse in our childhood.

At the suggestion of a counsellor friend I need to sound
a warning here. She felt that some people, unless they are
highly skilled in this area, may read the list of indicators and
feel they are now experts in diagnosing the presence of child
abuse in the majority of their acquaintances. She feared it
could be possible to subtly include too many non-abused
people into that category. So please use commonsense and
do not misuse this list. Though tempted, don't succumb to
a secret desire to play Freud. Hurting people need understanding and love, *not* to be categorised.

In sharing these indicators, I'm not saying survivors are strange, odd or incapable, nor am I denigrating them in any way. I don't wish to humiliate those who are already suffering. My purpose is to help others understand that very often we have ways of behaving which reflect our inner image of ourselves and pain from our childhood abuse.

Which leads me to make a plea for supporters to note, even though everyone has emotional difficulties, that it is the *exaggerated*, or even the *diminishing* expression of emotions and their *combinations*, *extremes* and *intensity* which can show underlying problems. Then we can learn to look beyond the combination of presenting symptoms for their cause, which is frequently that a troubled, hurting and sometimes hurtful adult now was quite possibly the object of abuse as a child and that frequently these indicators have been ignored or overlooked.

List of indicators:
1. Lack of trust: in other people and God. Suspecting peoples' motives.
2. Fear: recurring, sometimes overpowering, inappropriate for situation. Dread of losing control. Helplessness.
3. Worthlessness: feeling of being of no value. Self-hatred. Self-denigration. Overwhelming inadequacy. Constant apologising ('Sorry! I'm so stupid').
4. Guilt: without adequate basis. Unreasonable. Exaggerated. Irrational.
5. Shame: sense of degradation without known cause.
6. Seeking approval: excessive. Insatiable. Overly trying to please.
7. Insecure: unstable. Fickle.
8. Bitterness: internal isolation. Inner feelings often kept secret.
9. Love: difficult to give. Afraid to receive love.
10. Ignoring limitations: inability to cope. Physical

exhaustion. Pushing selves too hard. Acute fear of failure.

11. Taking the blame constantly: in impossible situations. Expecting and accepting incorrect blame.
12. Blaming others: always right. Utterly rigid in maintaining own beliefs.
13. Argumentative: difficulty in controlling temper. Sudden eruptions of pointless anger, as if some arguments are a fight for survival. Rebellious.
14. Excessively submissive: resigned. Broken. Strong sense of rejection.
15. Indecisive: difficulty making up mind, especially in such simple matters as which clothes to wear.
16. Rigidity: overly efficient. Very proper. Stubborn. Inflexible. Rejecting.
17. Passive aggression: subtle provoking. Manipulative.
18. Internal conflict: inner personal discord. Discontented.
19. Anxiety: unreasonable worrying. Inner confusion, turmoil. Hopelessness.
20. Inappropriate speaking: constant talking. Too quiet.
21. Overly sensitive: taking offence. Very easily hurt.
22. Unaware of others' feelings: blunting of personal emotions.
23. Overreacting: incongruous responses. Impetuous shopping sprees and financial transactions. Irresponsible schemes.
24. Overreacting to own children: expectations too high for child to attain. Over disciplining. Over punishing to the point of cruelty. Not able to enjoy own children.
25. Hatred: irrational. Ashamed to admit it. Often extreme and directed towards opposite sex. Turned inwards on self.
26. Cruelty: uncontrolled. Calculated. Sadistic. Personal vendettas. Spite.

27. Problems in sexual matters: fear. Distaste.
    Promiscuity. Deviant.
28. Dread of going insane: frenetic activity of mind.
    Excessive emotional pain.
29. Suicidal tendencies: need and desire to escape from
    self, others and/or circumstances.
30. Physical manifestations: drug, medicinal, alcoholic,
    other dependence. Anorexia nervosa, bulimia, obesity,
    other eating disorders.

It's remarkable, yet suddenly we see the relevance of
indicators like a light switching on. A doctor in her early
fifties explained what happened for her: 'Before I knew
about your indicators, there didn't appear to be many of my
patients who had been abused. Now when I notice in a
patient a combination of indicators, especially if they are very
extreme, I gently ask, 'Were you abused as a child?' Sometimes the patients withdraw into themselves; more often they
are very grateful and relieved to be able to share with me
that they were abused and how they are still being affected
by that abuse.'

Some supporters may think this approach is too confront-
ing. I, too, had doubts, until a survivor friend was
approached in this way and was thrilled that her companion
was 'clued up' enough to ask her. My friend was then able
to share freely much of her pain. I have no doubt, though,
that in this type of situation the great need is also for kindness
and discernment. Perhaps the question can be asked oblique-
ly. It seems to me if supporters do not ask, then who can the
survivor safely share with?

As I move through this book sharing the steps, the
indicators will come up time and again, because they have
become my lifetime behavioural patterns, my defence
mechanisms, my means of coping. So supporters, in your
desire to help us, I hope that by using the indicators you will
be able to discern if survivors are still suffering the results of

abuse in their lives and then be astute enough to direct us to have appropriate intervention therapy.

Before we begin the steps I took towards my ongoing recovery, let me say some things about them. First, they are the particular path I took. I know for many there may be another way. I hope they may be of value to you in your journey.

The second point is that you don't have to pass a test or get any step right before you can move on. You can start any place and move backwards or forwards. They overlap, interchange and flow into each other. You don't even have to be enthusiastic; the steps can be done in any mood.

For me there are days when the steps seem illogical, just sheer hard work, and I resist doing them or become indifferent. They seem pointless random actions, until a moment comes and I discover a pattern forming, my life expanding – becoming more real, more sharply etched, more deeply felt, whether it be sorrows or joys, pain or pleasure.

I find to my relief that I am beginning to move out of the extremes of my indicators, out of the emotional hell I lived in. I'm functioning differently. I'm leaving my past and breaking through into a new future.

PART THREE:

STEPS TO RECOVERY

13

My first step:
Listen to me!

THE MEMORIES OF THEIR ABUSE and their view of themselves usually seem to be the most painful place for many survivors. Equally devastating for me was my hostility to God, the sense of being separated from him.

'Why did you start your steps with this religious stuff instead of the place where it hurts me most – the pain from my childhood abuse?' Shirley, a survivor friend, demanded to know. 'That's where I need help.'

'Shirley,' I replied, 'I did the steps the best way for me; there's no special order. I started with God because that's where the big problems were for me and lots of abused persons. If I'd suggested you start by trying to change yourself, I'm not convinced that it would have done any good. That's why I began here to find out what God would do if I was honest and told him what I thought and felt about him. I needed to know whether he was dependable, if he'd really listen and how he would act.'

Words to a friend were one thing; actions were quite another. Could I admit to God all the things I really felt about him? I blamed him! Why hadn't he helped me? Why? I was hurt beyond words. And it seemed God had just stood by and let it all happen. All that abuse and all

127

those years of feeling like I was an utterly rotten person had produced in me so much suffering and a fierce hidden antagonism.

'I'm often opposed to God,' I blurted out to a friend one day, then wished I could snatch it back.

I waited apprehensively for her reply. To my surprise it came quite casually: 'That's right, of course you feel opposition to God. Everyone does at times, whether they admit it or even care about it. That's the way we are.'

What a relief! Her next statement amazed me even more: 'Do you know, you can tell God about being opposed to him. You can tell him what you really think and feel about him. You can tell him whatever is in your mind.'

This stopped me! Wasn't this going a bit too far? I knew some of the things I thought about God and they didn't seem too 'Christian' to me. 'Try it!' she had rather forcefully suggested.

This was a different approach! Not only was it different: it struck me as irreverent, even dangerous, to admit my hostility to God. I knew once I started, all the emotions I'd bottled up inside me for years would explode at God. I'd let fly how angry I was with him, that I didn't believe he loved me and that I didn't trust him to look after me. I'd pour out my fear of him and even my hatred. I knew I'd have questions and complaints, deep hurts and utter despair with the frustration of it all. And I'd demand to know why he hadn't rescued me from my abuse and my own inner torment.

What a collection of problems I'd tell God about if I started! But now at least I knew why I felt so badly about myself: the ghastly recurring memories of my parents' abuse explained that. Abuse and the adaptions I had made to it had corroded my internal life and secretly filled me with an overwhelming desire for death – anything to escape the nagging pain from my ceaseless private self-denigration.

'Try telling God,' my friend had insisted. At least here

was a new twist. I'd tried to confide in close friends that I felt no good and had strong internal hostility to God. Usually, whenever I had the courage or sheer despair to admit to such a thought, I was told: 'That statement is not doctrinally sound. You are not antagonistic to God. He has reconciled you to himself.' While my status with God is that I am forgiven, I knew how I felt and often there was little peace; rather there was confusion and hostility in me towards God.

So what did I have to lose? Could I feel any worse than I had for over forty years? Now was the time to take my courage in both hands and tell God how I really felt about him. No more putting forward the person I thought he'd like. No more pretending. God knows all about me anyway, so he must be aware of how I feel about him. Yet I still thought I was presenting a good face and maintaining a certain 'Christian-stereotype exterior', desperately endeavouring to love God and believe what the Bible said about him loving me, but feeling quite the opposite. Now that mask had to go. It was just God and me – and I was frightened!

Why so scared? Didn't I really believe that God loved me irrespective of what I thought and felt about him? I had firm Christian beliefs, but they were not touching me where I was hurting; they were not coming to grips with my reality. Though I believed in my mind that God could be trusted, in my emotions another truth remained: I felt I could not trust God no matter what my mind believed. My beliefs were not altering my doubts, my fear of God, my anger, my inner pain, or the fact that there were times I felt I hated God. What I believed with my mind was not altering how I felt.

So I started right there and told God every day as much as I could, more than I thought I'd ever have the courage to tell him. Is telling God a way just to accuse him? No! It simply stops me trying to hide behind my religious exterior and openly confess my real feelings about him.

When I began telling God, it had initially been just open

reproach, a device for relieving my pent-up emotions. Now I can see another element has been evolving: telling is opening up contact with God. I'm not just talking *about* God: I'm talking *to* him. I'm no longer secretly angry with God, but frankly admitting my reactions to him as honestly as I can. It's like opening a door which was tightly locked in me and now we can both go through it: there's a two-way interaction.

While trying to find answers from God in the Bible, I came across these astounding words from the Book of Isaiah: 'Review the past for me. . . let us argue the matter together.' What an offer from Almighty God!

I accepted. I reviewed. I argued and have continued to do this ever since. Even though I was afraid, sometimes I was so angry I just bombarded God with the heartbreaking questions which plagued me: Where were you, God? Why didn't you help me when I was being so mercilessly attacked? Didn't you love me? Didn't you care? Yes, I argued. I was angry with God – hurt and confused, filled with apprehension. Yet why such fear? Why was I so afraid of a God I'd been taught was essentially loving?

Who was your model for God? Did you have a father figure who loved you and was caring and reliable? How were you treated by the person who represented in your childish mind the attributes of God? My model was my father, a capricious, cruel sadist whose great delight was to torment me and use me. I knew I could not trust my father. Could I trust God? Was God like my father, just waiting to hurt me? How could I trust a God who was out to get me? And now I was placing myself even more into his clutches! I was planning to tell him that he was cruel and vicious.

I told him! Was I struck by lightning or did I have some other awful thing happen to me? No! Did my whole view of God change suddenly and forever? No! But a vital new knowledge began to grow within me. It happened unhurriedly but decisively when I found the courage to admit that I was afraid of God and, because of this, I could not trust

him. Even feeling this way I had asked him into my innermost being, which had previously been locked to him, to
work there and overrule my concepts. He obviously listened
and responded because I realised a wonderful truth. . . *God
and my father are not the same!*

God as a heavenly Father is not like my earthly father or
any other man. God is not waiting to play some diabolical
trick on me – he is not planning to hurt me. I no longer had
to live with the consuming fear which equated God and my
father. All my life I had superimposed my father's corrupt
nature on to my view of God, leaving little place in me where
I could believe the true yet difficult fact: that God longs to be
a dependable father, if only I will allow him. My longing is
for him to be the father I've always wanted – one I can trust
and love, not one who fills me with a fear beyond imagining.

The view I held of God being the same as my father had
resulted in a frightening ambivalence, a confusing love-hate
relationship. Holding apparent opposites in balance, always
a problem for me, had to be faced. On the one hand, I read
that God can be trusted – and I wanted to know this as a
reality in my life. On the other hand, there was what I
experienced in my emotions – how I felt about God because
of my assumptions that he was the same as my father.

Slowly this merging balance of mind and emotions is
producing a growing harmony and wholeness in me, even if
sometimes something from the past triggers my old fear of
God and I begin to panic. At last I know I don't have to
follow my usual strategy, persuading my feelings that I really
do not fear God. I don't have to change how I feel or
override my emotions. I can tell God how afraid of him I
am because of the memory of my father's cruelty. I can learn
once more that God and my father are not the same. I can
begin to allow a new concept of God to take hold and
develop within me.

As I became more aware of my father's ill-treatment and
told God what this had done to my relating to him and other

people, another devastating emotion became evident. More clearly in my conscious mind I recognised that *we who have been abused do not trust*. We have no basis for trust, we had no foundation in our childhood on which we could build trust. Our trust was violated as children, never allowed to develop in a normal manner.

I heard a teenager speaking about being badly abused by his foster parents: 'You lose trust – it's like losing your arm. You can't get it back,' he said, half in tears, half triumphantly. 'But I'm learning to cope.'

Basically I did not trust God or people. Of course, over the years I have learned to trust certain people: those with whom I'm involved can be trusted. But beneath that acquired trust is a place of no trust. Even if I'm not always aware of this state within me, it cannot avoid disrupting my life and profoundly disturbing my relationships.

At a crucial time for me as I was trying to come to grips with the fact of my inability to trust God and people, a friend's letter arrived. She dumbfounded me by saying: 'I don't trust God enough. How do you manage to trust him so much?'

Wow! What an extraordinary thing for her to think! In my reply I wrote: 'I feel I don't trust God much at all and yet I want to. So I've told him about it and I'm learning that this is who and how I am. This non-trusting person is really me. I am a "non-truster". My desire is to trust God, yet basically I'm a person who finds it very hard to trust him.'

My letter continued: 'Strangely, there's great release in admitting that lack of trust. I can rest in that, draw in a big breath, let it out slowly and admit: "Yes, Lord, this is me. After all you have done for me – all the things you've taught me, all the prayers you've answered. Even though I can look back and see how you have brought good out of evil, I can *still* say: I don't trust you, God."

'But you know,' I continued in my letter, 'I don't think it's really a terrible admission. What I'm saying is: "Here is my position with you, God. This is the truth about me; you always knew it. It's me who keeps clouding the issue, wanting to have my own private stock of faith, an 'accumulated trust' which keeps growing and which I can call 'all mine'. Then I guess I wouldn't need to depend on you, God, to teach me, love me and forgive me."

'So every time I fail to trust I try to remember to tell God about it. I try to see that this is where I'm coming from because I could not trust my parents. I can't just turn "trust" on automatically.

'God does not seem floored by this. He stays constant even when I admit my "seesaw" trust to him. . .'

Facing my whole attitude of not trusting God awakened another problem of much heartache in me. I seemed unable to envisage either a good father or a good mother who could be trusted. It had been hard enough to acknowledge my father's cruelty. But now I had to face untold horrors about my mother. The common ideal of motherhood is that mothers are kind, loving, nurturing, protective. Unfortunately, this is not always the case.

My own mother was a confusing and frightening mix of trying to care for me while also being cruel and failing to have the slightest regard for my well-being. Occasionally I'm still caught in the nightmare of remembering, yet not wanting to believe that my mother did not even want me; nor was she kind or protective. She rejected me while, in her own peculiarly twisted way, maintaining the facade of loving me.

In fact, her collaboration with my father in his deviant sexual molestation filled me with anguish and incomprehension. These questions keep troubling me: How could a woman set her own daughter up for such degradation and agony? How could she leave me to face alone the violence of my father's uncontrollable lusts and anger?

I've found myself begging for answers which I may never find. How does a child cope with such rejection, such betrayal? How does the adult with that in her life cope now?

At times my fear of betrayal, through all the subtle ways it manifests itself, almost overwhelms me.

Slowly I'm beginning to comprehend that because my mother rejected me, it does not follow that God will reject me also. And on that basis, because my mother rejected me, can I reject God? If I did, where else could I go? To cut myself off from God would leave me destitute.

One way I've found to ease my misery is to pour out my anguish to God: with tears and pain to share it with him and ask him into that place in me where I hurt so much. This allows him to steadily alter my lack of trust and ease the pain from my parents' rejection. I'm learning, falteringly, to ask him to forgive them. To wait for his restoring. To begin to trust his words, irrespective of how I feel that, even though my mother and my father forsake me, God will take me up.

Again there is a holding in balance of my mind and emotions. Gradually growing stronger in me is a well-founded hope that, one day, I will be able to accept God as a trustworthy parent: a gentle caring mother, a strong reliable father.

But just as I begin to think there may be a small breakthrough, a move at reconciliation, I'm set back, restrained by remembering another huge problem for me and for so many survivors. It is our belief that God failed to help us. What suffocating, heartstabbing rejection we feel from this, too. God's visible failure to help again and again at our times of childhood crisis is a cruel, unfathomable mystery for me.

I've had some survivors yell at me in a rage: 'God can't be trusted. Where was he when I needed his protection? What's your answer to that?'

I don't have adequate answers. I must leave the answers to him. What I do know is that God is beginning to use my pain constructively. God is using the suffering I endured in my childhood to help others and me. There's a sense of compensation in this, a warmth even, which somehow eases the coldness of my terror and rejection as a child.

Even with all our pain, we survivors can make workable choices. We do not have to continue on helpless and hopeless as we did as children. We do not need to feed our hate, heighten our anger or live distrusting others. We can tell God about our anger and hate towards him. I know women survivors who don't just tell God; they yell, shout, stamp and scream at God. I did that! I believe God listens, even if coherent words are beyond us.

Yet it is absolutely imperative that in the long term we are *not* controlled by our anger and hatred – that telling God, and our way of doing it, does not become a hate session and we are not dominated by these emotions until they become the driving force in our lives. Some survivors choose to do just that. But I have watched hate and bitterness 'eat up' lovely people until they became cold, hard and vindictive, growing more hurt by their own hating.

Somehow it all has to do with our attitude. We have a say in whether we want to continue with our lives full of hatred, or we can ask God to change us. Basically what I did about ten years ago when I started to tell God was to ask him to overrule my hatred. This is another big step towards my recovery.

'After you'd suggested telling God what we felt about him, I figured I'd give it a try,' Shirley told me. 'I was wondering how to get his attention. So I stood quite still in the back garden, with nothing between me and the open sky, and I yelled, "Listen to me, God! I've got something to say to you!" So I told him, "I hate you and I hurt!" I said it over and over. It felt so good to be able to tell God that at last.'

After a few quiet minutes, a slight grin crossed her face and she exclaimed: 'I got a helluva shock, though, when a loud voice suddenly said: "Were you calling me?" Thank goodness it was only my neighbour!'

It is a strange fact that, even though we find it extremely hard to trust, a great deal of our living is based on trust. I find myself trusting God and others even if I don't know I am. We do it unconsciously. If public facilities such as electricity, water, buses, trains and shops ceased to function, even in their partially reliable way, our country would grind to a halt. Yes, we do a lot of unconscious trusting; other people can usually be trusted to be there if we need them. Yet sadly for survivors, there is a sharp underlying fear that our trust will be betrayed. When we can't trust or are afraid to, our lack of trust plays havoc with our relationships. Often we are on guard, afraid to trust even those closest to us.

This is not easy for our supporters. The inability of survivors to feel they can trust is one of our most painful indicators, causing problems for those who want us to know we can rely on them. I'm often told by supporters that our lack of trust produces a sense of helplessness in them.

Though what I'm about to say may seem a backward step or even go against what supporters want for us, I suggest you try to accept that we are conditioned not to trust and that it is neither your fault nor ours. Fighting against it, denying it, trying to persuade us to trust: none of these will ease our non-trusting. Paradoxically, your acceptance of it as fact will begin to set us free to deal with it. So please allow us to admit that we do not trust.

One of the most freeing and renewing experiences of my life was to know I was still accepted when I finally admitted to God and to another person that I didn't trust people and I did not trust God. This acceptance somehow gave me an opening, permission as it were, to deal with my problems and the courage to go on and face more of my pain. Because acceptance did so much for me, I'm asking all who love us and want to help us: 'Please accept us and endeavour to believe what we are sharing. Try to comprehend not only the words we speak, but our inner pain, which we may be finding difficult to explain. Don't try to stop us expressing our negative feelings. Don't deny or decry our lack of faith, or our inability to reconcile God's words with what we feel deep inside. Let us acknowledge it, bring it out! Let us share it with you and Almighty God.'

I believe that Christ died not so he could break us, but rather so he could break us *out* of our prison. My desire is not to give up or give in, but to show that God can and wants to work with what I am, who I am and how I am, and that I can choose to be open and allow him to make the necessary changes in me.

How hard it was, and still is, for survivors when we were unable to trust those people who were meant to look after us! A very dear, yet so cruelly abused survivor friend received a wonderful gift recently. For several days her joy seemed complete. Then the old fear began to strangle her again. 'It won't last,' she told me with heartbreaking resignation. 'I know something will go wrong and it will be taken from me. God will not let me have it.'

Oh the pain, the rejection in that, the awful fear straight from her abused childhood. 'Tell God this is how you really feel about him,' I whispered as I cried inside. What else is there for one so hurt, but to share it honestly with God?

Originally when I'd first started to tell God how I felt about him, it took all my courage, then usually I blurted out angry retorts filled with pain, fear and resentment. Too frequently I was censuring God. But now my telling is changing. It is much wider, more of gratitude, even love – and concerned with the needs of others. And to my surprise more time is spent listening and waiting.

One evening, my husband came up behind me chuckling: 'Told you so! At last I've caught you talking out loud to yourself.' I couldn't deny it! At the moment I was caught I was engrossed by the view from my window, swept up by the wildness of the sea, whitecapped and racing. The truth was out. It had become such a part of my life I hadn't noticed that I'd been talking out loud with God, mostly grieving with him about those children of our city who had no shelter on this wild, cold night.

'Oh God, my whole being cries out for those who are destitute: many without food, homes or love, even the simple things of life. I wonder do you care, God?'

I am beginning to realise that God cares much more than I ever could, that he wants us to rely on him, but often we fail to ask or believe this. Or he calls us to do something about this world's heartaches and we fail to hear and act. I'm learning many things by telling God how I feel about him. It's a worthwhile step to take what I believe he hears, honours and answers, albeit in his own way and time.

Recently I received a letter from a young social worker who is trying to cope with the after-effects of being sexually molested as a little girl. 'Well, I've got your steps,' she wrote, 'and after six months I'm still stuck on the first one. I just can't get past it. I keep telling God and telling him what I think of him.'

Don't stay stuck on any of the steps. If you stay on step one you could atrophy right here. Having started telling God there's no point in stopping, because telling God is just that – a first step, the beginning of a whole new movement towards him, the start of a different relationship. You've only just begun what can become a great adventure with God. Get ready to move on. Yet don't stop being honest with God.

Telling God – asking him – has opened locked places in me, showing me that I wouldn't have the courage to ask or tell him anything unless somewhere in me a small seed of trust had taken hold and was putting out little tentative green shoots. One day it can be healthy and flourishing but, like me, it still has a long way to grow.

Growing with God and using the steps goes on for a lifetime. If I live till I'm ninety, I expect to continue working busily with God on every area of my life.

14

My second step:
This is me!

'I'M NO GOOD! Just no good! Why was I ever born?'

Even over the phone, Jane's abject misery engulfed me. I wept. Yet I had to let her tell me. I had no doubt she felt this badly about herself, because those heartbreaking words were mine, relentlessly echoing my pain-filled daily beliefs about myself. I was 'no good!'

Being abused as a child had done its terrible work only too well. It had distorted my view of myself. This wrong image had contaminated my life. It swaggered through the years of my story, pouring its torment, its contempt over every page.

'If you only knew me,' Jane stated. 'If you only knew me like I do, you'd know how worthless I am.' Jane was experiencing one of those devastating times of depression which intrude frequently into the lives of most adults who were abused as children. She is a delightful young woman: caring, intelligent, lots of ability – a bit fiery perhaps, but this adds to her courage and struggle to keep going. In fact, there is little correlation between how she perceived herself and the person we all know.

We survivors see ourselves differently from the way others see us. We read our world differently from the way others do.

For years, I'd been listening to my pitiless self-recrimina-
tions and trying to explain my internal horrors to
psychiatrists and others. My faithful family and supporters
had tried to help. But they had not been able to comprehend
the extent of my anguish nor why, because I appeared to be
coping. They could not see the wretched inner misfit I
believed myself to be. There was no deception in my contradictory images. I really thought it must be obvious to
everyone what a horrible mixed-up person I was inside. I
was persuaded in my mind that they knew about me, but
were too polite to tell me.

These prejudiced conclusions, though incorrect, made me
feel even more cut off from others, because I was convinced
they could not possibly like me. But I was so in tune with
a desolate survivor who said: 'I need someone to tell, somewhere to go, where I can be the broken person I am.'

God was becoming that someone for me. Since I'd been
doing the first step, I knew God was responding, changing
our relationship. So I decided it was safe to push on and
have a go at this second step, too. God already knew my
secret inner truths, though I had never opened myself like
this to him before. Here in this step was a different strategy,
a whole new way of relating to God by telling him what I
think and feel about myself. I don't understand how it
worked, yet to my surprise the debilitating anguish inside me
began to ease.

How I needed that! I'd been trying for years to escape
from the vice-like grip of my strangling inner beliefs. Now
the incongruity was that, instead of following my usual plan
of escape, ignoring them, pretending, hoping they would go
away, or fighting against God and myself, I was deciding to
shout out loud – tell God – 'I'm no good!' And in so doing,
I was looking at my horrors, facing them and openly acknowledging their insidious control of me.

But I could not begin to imagine how honestly telling God

that I felt as awful as I did about myself could possibly be a
step towards recovery. It turned out to be just that! The
answer lay in who I told, not just the telling.

At first I found telling God very difficult; now it's not as
hard as it was, though occasionally there's a perverse streak
in me which still resists telling him anything at all, or I just
become indifferent to him and the whole concept. When I
started being open and honest with God, I wondered what
would come out. Would I tell God that I was fiercely angry,
deeply hurting? That there were days I'd been wiped out by
self-hating depression and wished I'd never been born, nights
consumed with nameless terrors when I'd desired death?
Yes, I'd need to tell him all that and more.

'God, this is me. This is how I really feel. This is the truth
as I see it about me. It's one thing to know it inside me and
quite another to express it openly to you. It makes me very
vulnerable. I'm afraid of that, scared of letting you too close.'
Nevertheless, I was determined to tell God what I believed
about me.

Most survivors I've discussed with, read about or heard
speak have characteristic problems in common as a result of
their abuse. Yet they don't feel the same; their reactions vary
in intensity. What I am describing is how I felt.

A word forced itself into my mind and out through my
reluctant lips. A *thing!* My parents had treated me as a
thing. Apparently a feelingless object, not a person to them,
of no more value than other things they possessed and used.
Many survivors tell me they, too, have this degrading evaluation implanted in them by their abusers.

One of the horrors of abuse is that at some stage victims
agree with what we assume is the assessment of our abuser:
that we are of no value. Only a thing! We rationalise that it
must be so, otherwise why would we have been debased in
such a way? Frequently we are the ones accused of being
the evil influence in the abuse. This exerts such power that
we are largely incapable of breaking that control from

childhood; we carry it with us into our adult perceptions of ourselves and our world. Also the awareness that we are disapproved of to such a degree can be extremely debilitating. Add to this our personal disapproval of ourselves and our energy levels can drop even lower, causing us often to feel very tired or even swamp us with chronic exhaustion.

The associations of fear, torment, sense of helplessness and evil still pervading our lives because of our abuser's power and our adaptions to that are like a magnet drawing us back. Sometimes it works subtly, at other times with ties too strong to sever by ourselves, even though we struggle to escape.

We need someone greater than we are to crash through the barriers of our assumptions about ourselves. I believe we need to learn how to transfer our allegiance from the disastrous domination of our abuser into a growing collaboration, with God in control.

It seems there's a choice here. Which would you prefer to be? Shaped by God or your abuser? Perhaps you may consider this question too simplistic and toss it aside. But the rest of your life can hang on your answer.

Even though we decide for God, just making a decision does not bring about an immediate life-renewing change. There will still be an immense amount to be done in our growth. Nevertheless, choosing is a good place to start.

There is no doubt I needed to be set free from the control of my past, conscious and unconscious, because it ceaselessly bombarded my mind with its cruel innuendos, or straight out accusations – that I was an evil person, stupid and hopeless, not as good as anyone else. I believed I was unlovable, that God and others did not love me and I was of no value. Had we recognised these feelings at the time, we would have known they were clear indicators of abuse in my childhood.

I was convinced I was a worthless person. All the loving words and actions of caring family and friends could not liberate me from the merciless clutches of what I believed to be the truth about myself. It was no good supporters telling me I was of value; in a sense you were too late. Worthlessness had been implanted in me from my earliest perceptions. Before I began telling God and my trusted supporters about these feelings, even the most ordinary things in my life were conditioned by what I believed was my parents' evaluation of me. Walking down a street could be misery, for I was convinced that passers-by, total strangers, were thinking: 'That woman is a worthless person!'

No amount of logical thought could shake what I considered to be this absolute truth. With much weeping, with suffering of body and mind almost beyond enduring, I told God about me. How could anyone put such extremes of anguish into tangible form? A torrent of words wrenched themselves from me, encapsulated in a poem of pain:

God, if it's true you cannot err,
how did I slip past your searching eye?
Elude your careful check?
Come into being?
> *What stopped you discarding me*
> *on to your 'not wanted' pile*
> *with all other rejects?*
> *Not fit to be!*
How could you permit the existence
of one, rotten inside,
hopelessly flawed?
A strange oversight!
> *When you made me a person*
> *could you not see?*
> *The failure – the worthlessness*
> *which would become me?*

You, God, are total truth.
All loving.
All seeing. All wise.
A faultless Creator.
> *Why, then, have I been*
> *through all of my life*
> *plagued by this dread secret?*
> *I am – a mistake!*

Seeing it before me, graphically portrayed in words, was my way of telling God. At last I could stare at those words which had previously been only gut-wrenching, destroying emotions and ask: 'My God, is this true? Did you make a mistake when you made me?'

Reason alone could not have helped me through such pain. God did. Out of it he is releasing, as if from the depths of that soul-shattering picture of myself as a worthless mistake, a gradually developing truer image. Yet it's strangely paradoxical.

I've found there's a big distinction between my feeling that I am of no value and God showing me who I really am in his sight. Irrespective of all the worthless feelings I may have, these cannot alter the fact that he considered me worth sending Christ to die for.

Over the years telling God about myself, trying to trust his word, learning about his forgiveness, using the steps have all been breaking down previously impregnable barriers in me, changing my image. So the poem took on a new ending, revitalising, freeing, reassuring:

I believe it no more.
Christ's scarred hands reach to me.
I created you, my child.
You are no mistake!

Sometimes I don't think we know clearly what we think and feel till we say it, nor do we always fully comprehend what we see till we have to describe it. The importance of describing myself candidly to God, with all its embarrassing truths, was opening new areas in my understanding of him and myself.

In one way I was encouraged and yet, in another, I was even more deeply distressed when I discovered that these devastating evaluations of myself were frequently the views other survivors held of themselves, too.

A letter I received expressed it in this way: 'Thank God for your courage in writing your book. At last I know I am not alone and not the despised leper I always considered myself to be: rotten to the core!' Who can comprehend the torment of believing such things about ourselves? Added to this was the subtle, insidious suggestion that this very rottenness embodied evil.

The ghastly story of my dear friend Lee's childhood is one of the worst I've ever heard. Her frightful ill-treatment still makes me gasp from the sheer horror of its brutality and sadism. Recalling the beginning of the search in her twenties to find the truth of her repressed childhood memories, she said, 'I had a driving force in me to get help. Even as a child my life was blocked – going nowhere. I didn't understand why. I couldn't remember having a bad life. All I knew was that I was evil. Terribly evil. I just had to get rid of that!' Of course, this friend was not evil: dreadfully hurt, yes, but not evil.

Everyone has their off days. My counsellor, whose patience had always impressed me, must have been feeling a bit exasperated with my extraordinary ability to take the blame even in ridiculous situations, for at one session she gave a huge sigh and wanted to know: 'Hey! Do you think you are the cause of all this world's ills?'

Well, I had to admit I wasn't quite that influential. Nevertheless, it seems taking the blame was part of the basic me.

For survivors, a most demoralising feature of our lives is that we often believe we are the one at fault for our abuse. I was quite sure that my parents' rejection and cruelty was caused by my own innate badness.

Usually we learn from an early age to blame ourselves, because offenders invariably project that burden onto their victims. Little innocent children are accused of being sexually provocative or made substitutes for failure in adult sexual relationships. Too often we're told it is the abusers' right to do whatever they want and that the children are without rights or privileges. If anything goes wrong, even pregnancy, it is the fault of the child or teenager.

We are trained to take blame. This carries over into the whole of our lives. I know a highly intelligent, extremely efficient survivor who is constantly apologising in situations where this reaction is completely unwarranted. What a clear indicator! We have learned to accept censure incorrectly where it is quite unjustified.

'Janet was killed last night in a car crash' was the tragic news I heard as I picked up the phone early one morning. She had been my friend for twenty-five years and was now my editor. I was stunned, shocked! Then equally as suddenly, I was totally overwhelmed by the thought that she had died because of her association with me. Yes, her death was *my* fault!

'Utterly ridiculous!' you would be justified in saying. 'Absolutely impossible!'

No matter how absurd it may seem, it was my genuine response. I've seen similar reactions too often in myself and other survivors to doubt the strength of our belief that blame is ours. We condemn and accuse ourselves constantly. I wonder if supporters can understand that we have been so set up, so programmed to take the blame that it is an habitual response from an abused person. Because this is how we are, it makes it easy for others, even those who love us, to let us be the scapegoat and unintentionally blame us.

Sometimes survivors can fall into the opposite extreme of unreasonably blaming others. We can become quite immovable, always right, as if being right in some way confirms our reason for existing.

I think many people, including survivors, also secretly blame God for our abuse or the suffering of our loved ones. We seem to have a penchant for accusing God. We are able to find a thousand reasons to blame him. These can be about anything from weather to war. Often it's easier to blame God or someone else, even someone we love, than to take responsibility for our own actions.

Parents who were abused need to watch this blaming pattern and not overreact towards their children by constantly condemning, over disciplining or setting expectations too high for them to reach. In due time with God's help and using the steps, we can learn not to blame others or blame ourselves needlessly.

Anger, though often heavily suppressed, is a menacing presence in most survivors. No matter how religious we are, it is there waiting to erupt unexpectedly, even violently, from unresolved emotions in us. While some survivors stoke the fires of their anger, others fear to allow it out of its straitjacket, still being caught in the terror of the retributions meted out for any angry display as a child, especially at the time of their abuse.

I believe it is essential that we admit to our anger and, together with its unhealthy accomplices of hatred and the desire for revenge, that we take them all out, look at them, face them, ask God to attend to them; otherwise they can boomerang back and hit us hard again and again. Supporters who accept we have these emotions and allow us to work with them will be greatly appreciated. So encourage us to come to grips with them, even though this may bring on powerful reactions. You will not be doing us any favours if you persuade us to squash them or act as though they will go away if we ignore them.

Kids can say funny things with great meaning. A friend's little daughter queried: 'If you hadn't been my Mummy and I'd met you somewhere, I wonder if I'd have liked you?' I wonder if we like ourselves? I don't think many abused persons do. This can have far-reaching effects because of a very disturbing truth: what we survivors believe about ourselves can have a powerful influence on our children.

Vibes flow between people. When we dislike ourselves, these vibes, whether true or not, often filter through to our children who take these as our evaluation of them. Yet this may be far from the truth. My own internal guilt, my sense of being flawed, unlovable and valueless flowed through my interactions with my own children, even though I thought they were wonderful, loved them and did my best for them.

But sadly the negative vibes can be the ones children adopt as their own, as though they were that unloved person. What guilt, shame and sorrow this can produce in survivors, yet in reality in this area, no blame is ours because the passing on of vibes happens outside of human control. Children are very receptive and can sense if parents are hurting, yet usually don't know the reason. They can instinctively feel they are the cause and accuse themselves.

Many take on an added burden, thinking they must support and protect the hurting parent. These impossible tasks can cause deeply felt, though unrealistically based guilt. Often they absorb much more from the parent's experiences; and suffering, often fear – stemming from the abused childhood of the survivor parent – may still be so strong that the child also lives in a very real terror which has no tangible basis in their existence.

Jim was a huge young man with a bright open face and frank eyes, strangely filled with tears. He loomed over me, dropped his young wife's hand which he'd been holding very tightly and crushed me in a big bear hug: 'Well, what do you know about that?' he grinned. 'I've always known it somehow! It wasn't me who was abused, but I sure had a lot of

those indicators of yours to worry about. It was my mum.
She was the one. Hell, what a childhood she had! I've been
getting her vibes since I was a little bloke [a size hard for me
to imagine!]. I always thought the whole thing was my fault.
It wasn't, but I sure felt guilty!' Sweeping his wife off her feet,
he twirled her around and, in front of a hall full of people,
kissed her with great enthusiasm, stating loudly: 'Gee, Love,
now we can get in there with God and do something about
it all.'

Had Jim's mother come to terms with her abuse, he need
not have suffered. When adults who were abused as children
are willing to face their abuse, the consequences of the
suffering which has permeated their family relationship and
flowed to society can be eased.

Sadly, sometimes there are more terrible results of abuse
than just our vibes being passed on to our children: there is
the actual abuse of children! We know that a proportion of
abusers have themselves been abused. I guess we also know
the disastrous fact that some abused women marry, or
partner, abusers. They often fail to help or intervene to save
their own children from being abused. Why? How can
they?

One reason I have found is if the mother's own traumas
are still repressed or have not been attended to, this can
shackle them so tightly that they become as powerless as they
were as a child being abused themselves. It distances them
from what is happening to their own children. The betrayed
become betrayers. Yet they are still responsible for their
actions in continuing the destructive cycle of child abuse.

Such a calamity, such lack of support can leave a child
feeling rejected, heartbroken and, possibly secretly, ferment-
ing with bitterness against the non-abuser, who is often their
mother. Both groups are torn apart by this betrayal and the
guilt, hatred, rejection and bitterness of these unresolved
hurts can encompass them in an impenetrable isolation.

If these, too, are not attended to, emotions so overpowering can lead to a terrible repetitive downward cycle which can continue to the grandchildren. A researcher found five generations of abuse in one family.

A grey-haired lady stopped me. It was a couple of hours since I'd finished speaking and was just about to leave. Looking very pale and exhausted, she said, 'I've waited till you were finished with everyone else.' Her eyes, red-rimmed, were holding mine as she continued: 'When I came I felt so helpless. Everything seemed hopeless. I was so ashamed. I didn't have the courage to ask anyone for help. You see, it's been going on for so long. I was abused, my daughter was abused and I've just found out my little grand-daughter is being abused. Oh!'

She wept. I touched her hand and we just stood. Then, straightening her shoulders she went on: 'I thought it would go on forever. But it doesn't have to now, does it? I can be brave for us all. I can get help. The cycle of abuse in our family can be broken. I'm going to tell the authorities. And I'm going to tell God and ask him to work in our lives, too. That'll be new for me!'

The cycle broken

How do I see them –
my beloved children?
Not abused, not degraded – as I was.

How did I see them –
my troubled parents?
Hurting and hurtful – were they abused,
too?

How do I see him –
my God acting?
So the past's not repeated – the cycle broken.

How will I see them –
my children's children?
Joyously free from that fearful heritage.

When this activity of telling God how I thought and felt about myself was new for me, Jane had demanded to know, 'What difference will it make?'

'I didn't have a clue what difference it would make when I started,' I'd admitted. 'I just knew I had to do something. I was at the end of my tether. Even so, I found it distressing, at times humiliating, telling God how I felt about me, because the truth about ourselves is often very painful. But knowing that truth is an all-important part of our recovery.'

'I suppose you'll tell me,' Jane had interjected, 'that everything is just great in your life now? No more guilt, no more damage from your abuse?'

'No!' I replied ruefully. 'Wouldn't it be great if I could? I can't. Everything wasn't "just great" then and isn't now. Often I feel pretty low, but not trapped like I was in my horrors. At last I can tell God about it all. That's the big difference!'

'Do you mean that you're not angry with God any more?' Jane wanted to know. I had to be honest with her.

'That hasn't all gone either; some of it's still there. It catches me at unexpected moments. The change for me now is that I'm sure God wants me to tell him when I'm angry and everything I feel. So he can do something with the whole lot. He actually wants to hear my attitude about him and myself. He doesn't want any platitudes or pious phrases: he wants the truth as I see it – unadorned!'

'Just like you're thinking it?' Jane queried, eyebrows raised.

'That's right!' I admitted. 'God wants me to be as honest with him as I can. I'm finding the courage to tell him there's still doubts and pain and hurt in me. How worthless I feel sometimes and how I've felt bitter and angry because I thought he had deserted me.'

'All that?' Jane burst out.

'Yes. The lot! That's what God wants to hear. Finding that out has really helped me. Telling God about myself, which includes my lack of trust in him, has somehow given him access into me. It's making it possible for him to unblock me and release me from the control of my abusers and their insinuations of my evil and worthlessness. At last he is able to come in and gently begin to repair my emotional and spiritual damage. By being open and honest with God, I'm beginning to know him and myself in a different way. And I don't have to be any other person than me – just who I am with all my faults and yet seeing and being able to slowly acknowledge the worthwhile attributes which are also mine.' Jane looked wistful: 'Would it work for me, too?'

'Yes.' It was good to be able to answer that. 'God is the same towards everyone.'

It dawned on me with surprised delight that telling God is actually praying. Praying is a two-way activity and God's response is the most important part. For years it felt as though I had a homesickness of the spirit and I'd been longing to return to him. Now it's like I'm coming home to God.

15

My third step:
Manage me!

DEFECTIVE NURTURE in my childhood had so undermined my capacity to trust, whether it was other people, myself or God, that it became necessary for me to ask God to take responsibility and manage me – to fill up the gap – for what was lacking in my ability to trust. I had been so opposed to God, so angry with him, because he did not seem to help me when I was being so ruthlessly attacked as a child, that I needed a strong remedy for such an overpowering problem.

In asking God to manage my life, I meant more than is usually meant by those words. Not just 'help me!' – we all need God's help. I was requesting him to take over, to direct me – to use his strength, his wisdom, his guidance and overrule my wants and desires. I was saying, 'I need you to manage all of my life's situations, but especially while I'm working through my pain; because somehow I have to trust you, God, *even when* I don't trust you!'

I'm aware that I had actually chosen to trust God. My difficulty was that I felt no sense of trust. Asking him to manage me is an expression of trust that is real, a way of making that trust concrete if not felt in my various experiences and circumstances. To ask God to overrule is a technique, making a deliberate choice in spite of my feelings.

When I first started using this step it was like a terrifying leap into more domination, but now I've found it's asking God to put into action in my life what he sees and knows is best for me. No longer is there the cool detachment expected as part of a manager and worker arrangement; instead, an intimacy and warmth is flowing through our relationship. It's as though I've given my assent to God to go ahead and work his way in my life. That assent includes my participation: I am still responsible for my decisions and actions.

My strong need for God's intervention led me to choose to use the word 'overrule' for this step. That's my personal preference. I'm aware it's a harsh, hard word and not at all popular. 'Overrule' has connotations of dominance, subjection and authoritarianism. These are not what I receive when I ask God to overrule. God is not dogmatic; neither is he soft. He acts *for* me, not against me. There is control and direction, there is overruling – all of this tempered by wise guidance and loving compassion which enhances my freedom, releasing me to more personal development.

I didn't know this would be the outcome when I first asked God to manage my life and I was very apprehensive. Taking a step like this with its association of overbearing control was, and still is, a problem for those who were abused as children. The women in our survivors group brought this out clearly.

'Overrule – not likely!' stated Shirley in no uncertain terms. 'I'll never ask God to overrule anything about me! That's what happened to me when I was little. I was overruled, overthrown, *overcome*! No way – I won't say that! I won't give anyone that power over me.'

'That's how I reacted at first, too!' I agreed. 'The word, the whole concept made me hopping mad. I didn't want to be overruled because it seemed to mean more submission, more helplessness. I'd had enough of being crushed and broken as a child. I wanted nothing to do with overruling.'

'So why do you do it?' Jane queried. The others in the

group nodded in assent, 'Yes, why?'

'Let me say, first, that "overrule" is my word,' I answered. 'It suits me! Yet there are many interchangeable words. It's the essence of this step that is important, not the name. It was essential for me to have help outside myself and I felt that God was the only one to give me that. Even with all my resistance to him, I had to find a way to have contact with him to enable me to deal with the difficulties of my life. I felt I was going to pieces, maybe insane. I knew I must have a way to put into his hands, quickly and concisely, all these horrors, all my inability to cope, all my failure to know what to believe: in fact, all my circumstances. When I use the word "overrule", he knows that I'm saying, "Show me how to act and give me your wisdom, guidance and control – and your ability to enable me to cope. Also produce your desired results."

'I was convinced I was making a horrible hash of being a Christian. Even though other people seemed to be doing all right, I knew I wasn't. I desperately needed a way to work in harmony with God.'

'But it's been over thirty years since you became a Christian,' Bronwyn remembered. 'What's happened all that time?'

'All those years I've not been able to live as I thought God wanted,' I said, feeling a bit embarrassed. 'I've prayed, I've asked for God's forgiveness and, through these, God has helped me and sustained me. Nevertheless, secretly I've had a continuous struggle. I've been walking two conflicting paths. On the one hand, I've wanted God's way and, on the other, I've wanted my way – with not much success either way. I knew it was essential for me to break that conflict and have an approach that worked in my relating to God.

'I remember years ago in a study group being told "to be more obedient, more kind, more hospitable, more loving". Others there were solemnly agreeing, but it was sending me deeper into despair. A young woman near me drew in such a big breath I thought she'd explode if she held it much longer, then she burst out, "I can't do it! It's no good! I try, but I just can't seem to do those things properly I'm told I should. I'll go home and feel even more guilty than I did before I came." That's how it was for me, too. I had trouble doing the things I knew God wanted me to.'

'Has that changed now?' Mary asked.

'Yes, but in a back-to-front sort of way, because there are so many occasions I need to ask God to manage me, this shows me I'll never be able to achieve fully what he requires. I'll always fail in many areas. There will always be problems in me. I'll always need to depend on God for his help and directing. But I've made, and keep remaking, a momentous discovery: *I don't have to succeed to be acceptable to God.*

'I know I want to be just right for my own sake but, when I admit to God I'll never be as I should be, I stop struggling. Then he can begin to change me and make me as he wants me to be. Asking God to overrule in my life then comes into its own because it gives God the freedom to mould me into his chosen design. It reminds me of a potter working and re-working the clay to make the article as he wants it. Of course that clay doesn't have any say. But I do. God has given me the option to have him work in me and take over.'

'*Take over*! Why would you want God to take over?' Shirley blurted out.

'For the same reason. I'm not able to manage my relationships and my emotional and spiritual life alone.'

'Well, we all know that feeling,' Jane frowned. 'However, I don't want to be clay.'

Like fireworks, the questions exploded fast and furious:

❏ **What is overruling?**
'It's a method of interaction between God and myself by which I ask God to intervene and have his control in every aspect of my life. God does the actual overruling in whatever

way he chooses for, in some manner which I don't understand, asking God to overrule gives him freedom to govern my desires, words, actions, reactions and my life.

'I can open every situation to him by just asking him to overrule. It's quick and easy to say and this enables me to readily participate in his plans for me, which I'm beginning to discover are not just arbitrary; they are careful, loving plans which God wants to bring about for my benefit and the benefit of my family, too.'

❑ Will overruling really help?
'Using it works for me,' I told the group. 'I believe it's got tremendous potential for good which I've only touched lightly so far. But, before I explain this step of having God overrule me, there's something I want to make clear.

'I think we survivors need to be able to admit if we don't trust God. When I do this, I find it's so much easier to ask God to go ahead and work in my life, knowing I have honestly stated how I feel things are between him and me right from the start.

'I've found asking God to overrule is absolutely life-changing. It does great things, yet it's not essential. Many people never use it. But for me, learning to ask God to overrule is proving to be the pivot of my spiritual rejuvenation, the centre of an unexpected adventure where God changes things about me I've never been able to change by myself. Yet I'm not falling apart; I'm coming more together. Overruling is really the *linchpin* holding together all the other steps I've been working on for the last ten years.

'I find it fascinating being involved in the exciting and innovative ways God is then free to work. Having God's direction produces some extraordinary insights which are singularly enlightening. But I must admit there are times I become indifferent or totally forget to even ask God to manage things for me.

'Recently I felt I was stuck in a spiritual bog. I began to

pray and explore it with God. Why was I stuck? Was there something I should be doing or not doing? What was happening? So I asked God to overrule me staying that way. I did this for a few days, then promptly forgot to do it again. Despite this, he did answer this request and it came in this way.

'I was angrily muttering about God that he doesn't always look after me the way I'd like, when suddenly a friend pointed out something I hadn't noticed before: "Well, you sure are in a rut! You always say God won't look after you, no matter what the facts are. You're stuck! Don't you know that?"

'It was too starkly true for me to deny. I was repeating something I'd been saying in my mind for fifty years. I was caught in my habitual thinking. Without stopping to think, I had condemned God. I had repeated a phrase, my mind had agreed to it, my mouth had said it and I hadn't even queried it. I felt ashamed.

'Then I became elated. Here was a first-class breakthrough! I didn't have to think the same old way again. Here was a whole new way to look at God and everything else. Habitual thinking had been controlling my responses. What this friend said about habitual thinking was true: "The more it happens. . . the more it happens."

'I wondered how much of my thinking was a bad habit I didn't see. At last I had a new freedom to examine it all, because God had heard and answered my overruling prayer and shown me this controlling thought pattern. Now, every time I'm caught by habitual thinking, I can ask God to overrule it. Staying stuck in my usual pattern is out!'

❑ **Are you suggesting we ask God to overrule, too?**
Shirley's anger was starting to simmer again.

'That's up to you. I'm just telling you about this step. I know it's hard. I'm not surprised so many people buck against the word. There's no other word that expresses as clearly for me that I want God to be in charge of my life, especially in critical situations.'

'I think it's a lousy word and a damned hard concept!' Shirley was furious by now.

'True! But it's not really the word we use; we can choose our own word. It's our attitude that matters,' I said.

Bronwyn said gently, 'I ask God to overrule sometimes, but usually I just ask him to work; that suits me.'

'That sounds like you, Bronwyn,' I told her. 'But as I said, I've been so opposed to God ('Me, too!' shot in Shirley) that I needed a strong remedy. There's no doubt overruling is that.'

❑ **Do we have a choice?**
'Absolutely! It's entirely our choice to ask God to govern us or not. We don't have to invite him into our lives at all; he has given us free will.

'It's always been a source of amazement to me that God appears to wait for me to invite him to act in me, as though he desires my permission before he will begin to work freely and openly in me. He doesn't push himself or his will on me. Yet he so easily could. I've discovered there is no coercion. He is seeking and waiting, ready and wanting to work in me. I have the opportunity to say 'Yes', 'No' or 'Wait'. I can even ask God to overrule me waiting too long, and so putting off having the guidance of his control at all.'

❑ **Why would I even want God to overrule?**
'Perhaps you won't want to, yet the more I use it and under-stand it, the more I think it's worth doing. It appears to me God's intention is for me to co-operate with him in shaping my life. He actually wants me to have a say! I like to think one of his reasons, especially for us survivors, is because we were dominated and pushed around so cruelly as children that God wants to let us share as fully as we can now.

'But of course his desire is that everyone joins him in

changing their lives for the better. God can be in my wants and hopes, my anger, my fears, my selfishness, my loves and hates; every aspect of me can be made accessible for him to manage for me.'

❑ **When do we ask God to manage for us?**
'Every problem, even every thought, can be the right time to ask God to be in control. I do it when I feel perplexed or don't know which way to turn. Another time is when I think I have everything going just right and, especially, when I want my own way, irrespective of what's best for everyone. *That's* when I need it most. I don't usually ask him to change my circumstances or other people – just me.

'Our supporters can also help us with overruling. They can get us to try it, then encourage us to stick at it. Perhaps we can persuade them to try it themselves. It's not exclusive to victims of child abuse, wonderful as it is for us. Everyone can ask God to overrule.

'I'd been giving one of my supporters lots of little prods to keep her asking for God's overruling. One day, when I'd been cranky and grizzling, she eyed me rather seriously. "Are you having God overrule all that?" she enquired, trying to swallow a smug smile.

'You may think personal relationships will break down if you ask God to intervene and superintend them. The opposite happens. Being willing to have God overrule my relationships makes me more loving and my living with others more workable. An unknown, not understood constraint is lifted from me because overruling is a great pacifier, especially in arguments.

'I find if I'm willing to stop long enough in my angry retorts or my efforts to prove my point, and quickly dash off to God an "overrule me wanting to win, hurt or prove I'm right", then I can watch as he alters the whole flow of the disagreement. I'm amazed how suddenly in full flight I can be calmed down and begin to see, sometimes even understand, the other person's point of view, or else observe how the situation takes on a whole different direction.

'Actually many times that's easier said than done, because often I don't want to ask. So I have that overruled, too. It's like a quick prayer and no-one need ever know that I am making a quiet private transaction with God for him to direct whatever is happening. When I have God's overruling, I can start a new way of relating. The other person becomes more loved, not less.'

Bronwyn added: 'I like that. It makes me want to over-rule more, yet I need to say: "God, I do want you to be in charge, even if I feel I don't want you to. So please help me to ask you to do it." I think I'm like the man who wanted Jesus to cure his son, so he said: "Lord, I believe; help my unbelief!"

'I'm finding a willingness in me,' Bronwyn continued in her reasoning way, 'to have God change me however he wants, even if it's a struggle. Not just having him help me with the emotional after-effects from my abuse, but also to manage my ways of acting which are part of being a normal person. I agree with Cathy Ann that God sees our attitudes and deals with these more than our actions and feelings. He can overrule and further alter my attitude to him. I think this will encourage me to keep on with this hard step.'

❑ **What happens if we don't ask God to overrule?**
'Probably not much different to now. For some people they may not think that matters. But for survivors, with all the horrors we've had in our lives and their devastating conse-quences on us now, I think it helps us to have God overrule the effects of our abuse.

'When we ask him to amplify our past and present, then to manage it all, this seems to open every situation for God's possibilities. It's incomprehensible, but the more I ask God to take over, the more alive and integrated I seem to become. Also, I realise how much more there is to do. It can be a long, often painful journey.'

'That's what I'm afraid of.' Mary was very apprehensive. 'Will we be secure? If we start asking God to manage, who is going to be in charge of our lives? God or us? I'm afraid I'll lose control of my life again, just as I did when I was a child. I had no control then over my abuser who caused me such lifelong damage. I don't know what will happen if I let God control me.

❏ **Will I be safe?**
'I think,' Bronwyn added, 'that the basic difference between God taking over our lives and ourselves or others being in control is that God can be trusted to do the right thing for us. I know survivors have difficulty trusting God. We still have doubts about whether he will do the best for us. That's why I think the thing to do, regardless of how we feel, is to move ahead with God.

'Trust, it seems to me, can only come when we make a move in the *direction* of trusting. We can never travel on a bus to our desired destination unless we step on board. I'm learning to let God overrule my lack of trust and not be afraid. I can still know and admit that difficult things will happen to me and my family. But I'm finding out more and more that God always acts for my good, no matter how it may appear on the surface.'

'Even if all that's so,' Mary anxiously asked in a voice that was beginning to rise, 'I'm really afraid I'll cease to exist if I ask God to overrule constantly, or even a little. What if I'm wiped out as a person? What if I become like some dehumanised robot?'

'Many of my fears were the same as yours, but the very opposite has happened to me,' I replied. 'No-one I know who has made a practice of having God manage their lives has become less of a person. Still, I must warn everyone that using this step can cause each one of us an unexpected and even traumatic upheaval. There will always be changes God needs to make in us, so things can often appear to get *worse* on their way to getting better!

'When I ask God to take over, I feel I'm saying: "Lord, please overrule so that I don't rob myself of what you know is most appropriate for me." God uses our willingness to be overruled to build us up, not to tear us down, even though at first this may not always appear to be what's happening.'

Mary then asked hesitantly: 'Is it like letting go of what's inside myself and then being open to letting God act *in* me?' Heads nodded.

'If that's how overruling is for you, Mary, then that's great!'

'Humph!' said Shirley, strongly disapproving. 'You're setting yourself up for *God* to grab you. I can almost hear him yelling "Gotcha!"'

'I've decided that's all right by me,' Mary replied, holding her own. 'I can't feel much worse than I do now; this thought of letting go and letting God gives me hope. But I am wondering about the negative side of having God overrule. It seems a bit like putting yourself down all the time.'

'Yes, me too,' Jane responded. 'I sense there should be another side to it all, so I can put my point of view, too, instead of being like a helpless victim again.'

'Thanks for bringing that up,' I replied excitedly, 'because I've forgotten to tell you about *having God overrule my opposites.*

'I've made the interesting discovery that there are *two* sides to overruling. I don't just mean God's side and mine; I mean two sides from *my* angle. Being able to put forward my point of view really takes the sting out of this concept of overruling! This is what I mean.

'When I ask God to overrule my schemes so he can reveal his ideas, at the same time I ask him to stop me from losing my creativity.

'I think I see,' Jane interjected. 'I'm a bit fiery and get angry pretty often, so *if* I was going to have God overrule my usual anger, I'd be able to ask that the proper anger I feel because children are suffering would not be wiped out.'

'Got it!' I felt elated. 'When I ask God to overrule my image of myself, I try to remember to ask him to stop me devaluing myself so I'm not overcome by feelings of worth-lessness. Then my image isn't too low or too inflated. It's like putting before God as many options as I can think of. This regulating of opposites is his way of allowing me to participate as fully as I can. Quite a healthy way to hold my life in balance!'

'It sounds like giving both sides to God opens up the whole thing and gives him a larger place to work in!' Mary was feeling encouraged.

'Can you tell us other ways that having God manage your life works?' Jane asked.

'OK! Sometimes I have pet phrases for some of the things I ask God to overrule. Here's one of my specials I've mentioned before. It's asking God to *overrule the influence of other people on me and mine on them.*

'A while ago I had an insight from God which I could not have thought up for myself. A close friend had been unhappy with me for several months. I was wracking my brains to discover the cause and, naturally blaming myself, I'd come up with lots of reasons why she was mad at me – all of them my fault. I was asking God to overrule and both she and I were praying about the situation.

'In despair one day I said, "Right God, I'll face anything whatever to get this worked out properly." This might sound heroic, but it was my usual "last resort" prayer. I also put in, "Please overrule my influence on her and her influence on me. Also ease my wanting her approval and give us your wisdom."

'My expectation was that I'd see a whole heap of things I was doing wrong and lots I wasn't doing but should be. But no! The most interesting fact dawned on me. It *wasn't* all my fault! I wasn't entirely to blame! Well, here was a change. I could stop taking the blame. Feeling encouraged I renewed my efforts, adding, "Lord, please overrule me taking the blame in this situation." What a relief to ease up on my self-accusations!

'I saw her several days later. She was happy, like someone released from a burden. She could hardly wait to tell me how God was working on a problem in her life which had been troubling her for months and how it was being resolved. Though I don't understand how, I'm convinced the fact that I was constantly taking the blame was somehow allowing her to put her feelings and anger on me. I was available.

'I'd never have worked that out alone. It was good to be a part of a restoring action where I could see the loving, tangible results of God's overruling working so clearly.

'Asking God to overrule our influence on each other can make a tremendous difference in family and other relationships. This doesn't mean I get them to change. It's the same as always. I'm the only person I own. I can't give God anyone else to work in, though I can pray for them. So I ask him to alter my attitude to them and how we interrelate. What a freeing thing to do! It sets them free from me and me free from them.

'A psychologist minister friend wrote the following to me: "With overruling you certainly have found a truth that works. This is much more important than abstract knowledge."'

❏ **Does overruling help in praying?**
'Yes, in lots of ways it's invaluable. It seems to get me into a proper attitude, too. Often I'm not sure what to pray for, so I can ask God to organise both sides of the situations I'm in or any decisions I have to make.'

❏ **God works without overruling, though, doesn't he?**
'Oh yes, he does. Overruling is for my sake. It adds an extension to my praying. I don't just ask God to satisfy my wants, treating him like a shop assistant dispensing goodies.

I would rather have what he wants. This way I can ask him to overrule how I act, how I'd like every matter to be resolved – even how I feel about myself. I can't see the whole picture; only God can see that. I believe he has a better plan than mine and the power to bring it about. It's only commonsense to ask him to manage every circumstance.

'It makes me laugh sometimes when I make my own assumptions about situations or other people, convinced these are right. What a surprise when I ask God to "overrule my summing up" to find it isn't how I'd figured it out after all.'

'Some of those appeal to me, ' Jane said. 'I guess there are lots of other ways you ask God to overrule.'

'Tell us about them,' the girls said. Shirley groaned in a loud aside, 'Oh no, not more!'

'Often I'm aware of an alertness in me as though my antennae are out searching in case peoples' reactions change towards me. I'm ready for an emotional "flight or fight". Do you feel this way, too?' I queried.

'Yes, often,' came their reply.

'When I'm anticipating events happening I've found if I ask God to overrule he does: sometimes right on cue; at others in his time. He eases the fears and panic which are lying just below the surface of my life waiting to burst out and envelope me, often at most inopportune moments. My well-hidden fear of not being able to cope in many areas of my life leads me to confess and have God step in. Then he can work as he chooses. For years a silent cry I've often sent up has been: "Please God, overrule. . . I can't cope!"

'This quick cry enables me to face all the different conditions life throws at me. I often look back and see how surprisingly well I've coped with something I was scared stiff of doing, because I've dashed off a desperate plea and I believe God has answered and helped me.

'I have plenty of other times that God works to manage my life in an amazing manner if I'm not too stubborn to ask him, though I'm sure these will make the hackles rise for some of us. One is, I ask God to overrule me judging and making accusations against other people. Another is that I ask God to overrule me "protecting my own self-interest". In other words, I'm asking God to stop me trying to protect myself from the evaluations of others who may disagree with my particular views, wants, desires, opinions, activities, plans, decisions, pride, habits and philosophy.

'It seems like an awful, endless self-annihilating list which, if strictly adhered to, could rapidly turn me into a total doormat. But the very opposite happens. If I ask God to overrule me protecting my own self-interest, those things which really will be right for me seem able to come to the fore. I don't become a doormat, but rather it gives God the freedom to bring about, and me to experience, God's best results.'

16

My fourth step:
Amplify it for me!

'MY MIND CAN NO LONGER SUPPRESS or find ways to avoid my pain. I know I am at a point where I must make the unconscious conscious and let it go – or go under! But how?' This was the burning question gripping Paul, a man at the end of his emotional resources. His letters lay open before me; I have his permission to share these with you. They are so well-written, so expressive of how it is or has been for many victims of child abuse.

Paul continued: 'This morning "the sickness" is really with me. The rain has done so much good and today is a gentle day, warm and growing. The very life contained in it emphasises my (internal) dead prison: pitch black, deep airless, hopeless – a dungeon that is senseless, illogical, irrational and incomprehensible to all except those who live there, or have been there. To some of you this place does not exist because it is not real to you. . .

'Your tape hit home so often, with so much for me to relate to: to identify as my truth as well, to empathise with; so very much "pain" to come out, but from such a tiny access. The physical pressure makes me feel as if my chest and head will explode. Choking, gagging, pressured to hold in – God only knows what. I find it difficult not to escape to the prayers that I have so often voiced – that God will not let there be a tomorrow for me. . . But I'll keep trying to find the cause of my pain. I have to get rid of it.'

To Paul and to all survivors I'm presenting a paradox, a way of coming to grips with our pain by not trying harder, nor trying to escape: in fact, to give *up* trying, take a step that seems backward, face our pain and ask God to *amplify* our past. I always try and work with God. No matter how I feel about him, I can still ask him to be in it with me.

I'm not offering an easy way, but it's one that I've worked on, struggled with and know that God is able and willing to use in my life. I call it 'amplifying'. It's another of those words I use to express what I do. When I use the word 'amplify', I'm asking God to bring what he requires me to know, from the past or the present, to the surface of my mind to make it clearer. Then I can ask him to work in it and I also participate as fully as I can. Many people use the word 'intensify' and others don't use a word, yet they are engaged in the same activity.

'Why bother?' was Shirley's comment as I talked with our survivors' group about amplifying our past. 'Leave well enough alone. Live for the present. Peering into the past won't help anyone. Sheer waste of time dredging up all that old stuff.'

'That old stuff,' Jane retorted, 'is stuffing up my life right now! My present is a mess because of my past: it's suffocating me; it isn't just over and finished. Its influence has seeped into every part of my life and I'm slowly sinking into a bottomless quagmire. Yours may be over, but mine hurts like hell!'

'Sorry! But like I said, what's the point of looking back?' Shirley stated. 'What's happened has happened. Make the best of now is my idea. Don't let the past affect you.'

'Don't let it! I can't stop it. It's still here, right here!' exploded Jane, pointing at herself.

'I am the sum of all my days,' quoted Bronwyn very

softly. 'My life has become a mathematical maze which I am unable to solve. That's why I think amplifying may be worth working with. But I'm afraid of doing it. What will I find now? The things I remember from my childhood are bad enough; I'm scared to find out what's causing the emotional pain I still feel. Will I be able to cope when I do?'

'From my experience I think you will be able to,' I sympathised. 'But it won't be easy. I'm never going to minimise that! Even as adults it can be quite devastating to face the emotions and memories that were hidden as children, because they were too terrible for us to cope with when they happened. But we can cope now, and we do. I know because I've been back there many times and come through. It's altering my life; a new me is evolving – combined with the hurt, broken me – into a whole person.'

'Do we have to think up all our childhood hurts by ourselves?' Mary queried. 'That doesn't seem too safe a thing to me.'

'If you have a supporter you can trust, get them to help,' I replied. 'But I'd suggest you ask God to work with you both, because he knows what's in our unconscious, so he is the safest one to choose which incidents need to be remembered and which emotions should be faced. After this I ask him to overrule these and respond from his perspective.'

'Well, that may be OK for you,' Shirley interjected, 'but I don't trust God.'

'I felt just like that, too, when I first started my steps,' I admitted. 'I told him lots of times I didn't trust him. I think because I was honest, God worked with that, so we pushed on and the concept of amplifying began to make sense and be worth doing. I believe the same thing can happen for you because God cares for you as much as he does for me.'

Mary spoke up again. 'We're all talking about this amplifying. But what is it?'

'It's a yell for help, a way to let God in and let me out,' stated Jane, very definitely. 'It's a word we can use to ask

God to go back into our past with us and do something constructive there.'

'Spot on!' I agreed. 'It's like a key to open a door in me that unlocks my past, so God can show me what's in there that's affecting my life now, whether it's sad or glad, painful or pleasant. Then we can do something about it. I've also found out *when* to ask. My feelings are like a barometer, noting any change in my "emotional weather". So when this shows something odd is happening in me which is producing inappropriate behaviour or problems that may be making me uptight with people or situations, I ask God to amplify the cause.'

'What does God do? And what do I have to do?' Bronwyn asked in her determined, yet gentle way.

'My understanding of it is like this,' I replied. 'God waits, yet quietly encourages me, till I see whatever it is that's causing my reactions or trouble now. Then I ask God to amplify it. That means, to make clear to my conscious mind the particular problems associated with my reaction, whether from the past or in the present. Then I wait while God begins to release or in some way bring to my mind the stored up emotions which are causing my difficulty. Then it's my turn again. I give God access into myself and ask him to overrule every aspect of the whole situation. That's what I do and how it works for me. Then God steps in again, and brings about one of those extraordinary solutions of his that begin to change me and my ways of relating.'

'While I'm waiting for God to answer,' shot in Shirley, 'do I have to just sit, like a lily on a dustbin?'

'That I'd love to see!' I rejoined. 'No, just keep asking God to amplify the problem and go on living like you always do. But watch what happens, because he will answer in his own way and time.'

'Does God wipe the whole of our past away and all its pain?' Mary asked hopefully.

'Maybe for some people he does instantly cure their pain.

He hasn't worked that way with me,' I said. 'My history will always be the same. I believe I'll always have the scars from my abuse. But the extraordinary thing is that God has been able to – how can I say it? – to somehow reorganise the consequences of that abuse in my life. I'm not controlled by it as I was before. I'm no longer torn apart by its pain, nor led about by my emotions like a dog on a tight leash.

'Asking God to amplify my abuse hasn't taken it away, but it has transformed it. God has altered its effects on my present situation. Now I'm slowly changing; I'm coping more easily and becoming more real. And to my surprise, God is even using my childhood's abusing for his purposes and, more incredibly, at rare times to enrich my whole existence.'

I looked around this little group of friends, each one of us still suffering as adults from the after-effects of abuse in our childhood, and thought how glad I was to have them to share with. But I could not leave them with what might have been a false impression of me, even if fostered unintentionally. I had to tell them that I had not 'arrived'. I most definitely was not a 'healed survivor'. I was still struggling with living: sometimes depressed, sometimes happy, yet aware of slowly and surely moving into a place within me which I am beginning to appreciate.

Not only were there days I wasn't even asking God to amplify things that needed doing, or diligently working on all the other steps; I was often amazed to discover that maybe as much as a week had passed and I hadn't even thought about doing them, even though I was fully convinced of their life-changing results. Why didn't I use them, I wondered? Then the reason hit me.

My mind could be very easily deflected from speaking to God by my family's needs, writing and ordinary routine things like cooking, washing, cleaning and shopping. Yet if while doing these everyday matters I give God my attention, he can weave in his dealings with me.

I know I've tried to cram my days with activity and my mind with other things, so I wouldn't be overcome by what was happening inside me. Often my mind seemed occupied with such trivia, so that I wondered what was the point of bothering to think. Yet I found diverting my thinking from God and my pain did not ease my inner turmoil, even if it seemed to help me for a while. It was merely a substitute, what I call just 'filler':

The clamour of the mundane fills my mind.
    Crowding each corner with the dust and fluff of
       valueless nothings.
The space for true understanding,
    deep contemplation,
       diminishes.
Each day's trivia encroaches
    into the area for thought,
       insidiously consuming.
Yet there is a higher mental activity,
    more worthy,
       achieved less.
Little space allocated, little time given
    for listening to
       the voice of God.

I think that the mind consumed with 'filler' may never discover what interests God, because it may never make space to listen. It's one of the many ways we have of hiding from ourselves and God.

When I told my survivor friends that I hadn't wanted to mislead them into thinking I had everything sorted out, Shirley wasn't backward in coming forward with her comment and the others gleefully agreed:

'Oh, we all knew about you. You're human just like the rest of us. Still, we know you shared the steps because you hoped they'd help us, too, the way they work for you. That's if you remember to use them!' Shirley quipped.

We began to talk about other ways survivors try to hide or escape from what is happening inside them. 'Some survivors become workaholics, needlessly over-efficient, or they never seem to stop talking,' Jane put in.

'And some act as though they are never wrong,' Shirley added, 'while others go on impetuous shopping sprees, or indulge in wildly impossible financial transactions and irresponsible schemes.'

'I know others,' murmured Mary, 'who fill their minds day and night with fretting, but never seem able to come to any definite decisions.'

'Some of the very saddest,' Bronwyn said, 'feel driven to alcohol, to excesses in drugs and sex and other incongruous activities, to quieten the crying within them. I think we need to do our crying out loud – supporters can really help us do this.'

'Like putting sounds or words to our feelings,' mused Jane.

'Well, I think supporters ought to know that it can be damned hard work as they face our traumas with us,' Shirley said with conviction. 'Because of my shattering memories and pain, I do some terrible weeping and share some mind-blowing revelations.'

'I've done that, too,' confessed Jane. 'It's ghastly. I've often wondered if I could possibly survive it all mentally, physically or emotionally. But I have!'

'For me, the pain from my abuse had seemed endless and valueless,' I said, 'but this new, facing-type pain has gradually became pain with a purpose. I knew, with God in it, that it would achieve something and eventually come to an end. That's why, as I worked with my supporter, I asked God to amplify and overrule everything that came up.'

'I guess supporters, especially those from our families who want to help us, will have their own emotional distress at our pain,' Bronwyn said with understanding. 'They may take a while to adjust and feel limited in what they can do, but it would be so good if they could begin to comprehend that we survivors come from a special hurting place that's not the same for non-abused persons. It's what you call our "different basic reference point of defective nurture". I feel what we need from them is some understanding of how it is for us and a desire to listen and love us, not judge us.'

'There's something I'd like to say to supporters,' said Jane, 'that I feel very strongly about. It's not to force us into sharing our traumas unless they can stay and face these with us, because they'll need to continue listening, believing and still accepting us – even if they are caught in our pain and cry, too. So if they can't face it themselves, they'd better be honest and encourage us to see someone who can face it right through with us.'

'I'd like them to be discerning in other ways, too, and not expect us to face our pain until we're ready,' mused Mary. 'Some survivors may never ever want to face it, or have to.'

'Well,' Shirley insisted, 'I don't want them to try to stop me facing my pain. There's a time for many of us when we know it's right to come to grips with it all. So when it's time for me to go ahead and face what I really must face, I need to know it's OK with my supporters.

'I read something I think's true: "To deny someone their pain is to deny them the right to grow." I don't want a supporter to push aside the pain I'm trying to face and share by denying its existence. They may think it's not wise or just not understand my need and, out of misguided kindness, try to stop me because they think I'm already in too much pain. But they should allow me to be the judge of that.'

'When we tell our story,' Bronwyn quietly broke in, 'there may be many discrepancies or inconsistencies, so I want my supporters to understand that this is probably me as a child remembering bits of my horror which as an adult I may have hidden for years. At this time we desperately need to be believed, even if supporters find it hard to accept what we are telling them. Also, I'd like to remember to thank them more often than I do, because I'm sure supporters are hurt, too, even the professional ones, by the stories of our abuse and the inhumanity of our abusers.'

'I'd like to tell you all a wonderful discovery I've made,' I said, 'if that's all right with you?'

'Can we stop you?' came Shirley's provocative reply. I pressed on.

'While I was recuperating from an operation, my friend Lee rang me faithfully every few days. I appreciated this immensely, as she was in distress herself. My recovery was slow and painful, so much so that I began wearing an electronic gadget strapped to my wrist to stop the sensations of pain travelling along the nerves to my brain. It was a device of many visible wires coming from a heavy little box which I had to carry with me everywhere.

'One day Lee rang and, after we'd talked for a while, she said in her delightfully off-beat humorous fashion, "Get well soon. . . Oh, but I don't suppose you'll want to now, not with all the attention you'll be getting showing off your wires and your little box." How astute! She knows the need and desire of people who have been abused to receive lots of affirmation.

'I used to have an almost insatiable need for approval. It is one of the most difficult indicators for survivors to live with. Without being aware of it, I used many unconscious and even conscious ploys and manipulations to get someone to meet that need. Of course, we all need affirming, but my lack seemed almost obsessive and overpowering. Such a tremendous need to be loved and accepted! So, very simply and often, I asked God to amplify and overrule my excessive desire for approval.

'Though I did not realise it, I was really filled with longing for my parents to love and accept me. I did not think I would ever come through the torment in which I lived. I wondered if I would ever wake in the morning without the insidious nagging and hopeless feeling of wondering how I could face my day, yearning for the approval I felt I must have to enable me to cope. I believed I was of no value. I seemed locked into the control of my parents' evaluation and rejection of me, and blamed myself for it.

'Now at last I know my need for acceptance by my parents cannot *ever* be met. I knew this in my mind as a fact before, but not with my feelings – not with the clarity and sense of absoluteness that I do now. Oh yes, it was always there and always the truth. My parents, deep down, did not accept me or love me. They did not even want me.

'But I would not believe this – nor accept it. I must have approval. I demanded that others meet this need. How can any person satisfy the insatiable – in some way fill that aching emptiness? It cannot be done! Suddenly I realised that wound cannot be healed, nor that longing overcome. It is how it is. It forever is!

'How strange to have the search of a lifetime over. Not because the end has been reached, the longed-for prize attained, but because truth and reality have stepped in and shattered the treadmill and removed me from the ceaseless, fruitless round of my searching. There is no end, there is no prize. My parents will never accept me. It's too late; the past is over and my parents are dead.

'God has many ways to answer a prayer. Do you see how he answered my prayer to have my longing for affirmation amplified? He has shown me that I wanted my parents to affirm me. They can never do that. They cannot undo what has been done, nor alter my external history. I needed to see that. To have its pain amplified for me, I needed to accept and understand the awfulness of their *non*-acceptance. Only then could I be set free from their control.

'Then I asked God to step in and overrule my longing for their approval – for him to somehow overcome my need for affirmation. He answered that in the same way – not by giving me more affirmation, but by showing me that *the need I had as a child for my parents to love, accept and affirm me cannot be met now*. In fact, that need can never be met; to long for it and search for it wastes my life.

'That knowledge is my prize. That truth is my freedom. What an answer from God! At last he can begin to fill that emptiness.

'When I shared this knowledge with a friend, she stamped out in a rage, yelling at me, "That's the worst thing you've ever told me." Later she rang, yelling again: "Hey! That's one of the best things you've ever told me."

'For myself I could move forward from that point. I no longer needed to blame myself or keep on searching. It gave me a new reference point to grow and work from. I began to realise that the affirmation, the approval and love God and others give me, can be accepted and enjoyed by me. I can now allow myself to believe they love me and throw myself enthusiastically into loving them.

'With this new freedom another insight is growing stronger every day. It is that my loved ones, in fact all whom I meet, are also free. The stranglehold I had on them is being broken. My need for my parents to love and accept me does not have to be met by others. They are now all free to love me or not, as and when they choose. At last I can receive and enjoy the approval of others.

'What a delightful way to live. I like it!'

17

My fifth step:
Speak to me!

IT WAS SCHOOL HOLIDAYS and Gwen's children had taken over the house. When her aunt phoned, the noise level made conversation impossible. 'Hold on a moment, I'll fix that,' said Gwen.

When she returned to the phone, her aunt was impressed. 'How quiet it is; what wonderful control you have over your family!'

'Not really!' came Gwen's reply. 'I'm in the wardrobe.'

I enjoyed that – then its implications in my own life jumped out at me. Not that I wished to hide from the noise of my children – though it was quite an attractive idea – but rather I felt strangely encased, as though I was locked into my own restricted ideas and prejudices, not hearing what God had to say to me from the Bible through which he speaks to me.

The Bible might have little importance or relevance, or seem outdated or difficult to some; to me, however, Bible reading is being revitalised. Having God speak to me through reading the Bible in a new way is my fifth step.

Let me tell you how. Sometimes there is a blockage stopping me from receiving God's messages. I seem to approach the whole undertaking with my own preconceptions already solidly set in place. It isn't necessarily that what I hold is basically wrong; it's more as though I always filter what I read through the screen of my own limited knowledge, trying to make it fit into my scheme of things.

I need and want a fresh way for God to speak through my mental confines, through my 'wardrobe' and teach me what he wants me to learn. Here is a great opportunity to ask God to overrule my set ideas, show me his concepts, alter my habitual thinking and then for us to move on together and further open my mind.

As I read a particular Bible passage, I try to discover what I think it's saying. What does it mean? How does it apply to me? Then I write down all the thoughts which come to me: all the thoughts, not just those which seem acceptable, 'clever' or proper. So much tumbles out onto paper.

I write how confused I am in some areas; I unearth all my doubts, queries and objections; I allow myself to admit how angry I am about some passages. I become impolite, cranky and argumentative when I disagree with what is written – and breathe a sigh of relief when my views coincide with God's! The fact that maybe God is on my side after all is beginning to take hold of my mind.

I am forcibly being shown what the Bible is saying to me specifically, not just what I've always thought it said. Sometimes my interpretations hit home; others miss out on speaking to me because I'm struggling to fit the words I read into my pre-held notions of their meaning and into those concepts I want to hear. I try to squeeze God's immense precepts into the restricting smallness of my limited thinking.

One Bible passage I often use is the Sermon on the Mount (Matthew, chapters 5 to 8). I believe this is God's blueprint of how he actually planned for us to be. I don't see this as the way I am – or, for that matter, how others are. We have gone off on our own paths, deviating from the specifications of God's original plan for us.

Several years ago I began reading Psalm 139 from this new

and different angle. I asked God to reveal to me clearly what he wanted me to learn from it. I was bewildered, hurt and strangely angered when the writer said these words: 'I praise you because I am fearfully and wonderfully made; your works are wonderful.'

Who, me? Fearfully and wonderfully made? At that time I thought I was a mistake. Not any good – worthless. I did not believe I was wonderfully made. In fact in one particular area, that of my sexuality, I believed an incomprehensible error had been made.

I demanded to know what God's mind was about my sexuality. Here I was, a long-married woman with three adult children, still troubled and still endeavouring to come to terms with being uptight and unsure about the sexual side of my life, yet at the same time knowing that it is completely logical for survivors to have problems with their sexuality. For there is a vast amount of fear, guilt, shame, bitterness and personal denigration in this area. The damage and pain caused from sexual abuse as children has left a legacy of suffering which is still affecting our lives as adults.

God has interesting ways of answering our prayers. He began to reveal to me a different aspect of my sexuality which I had not envisaged before, using a trusted doctor friend.

As we sat one day leaning on an old table in the shade amongst the shrubs in my garden, our friendship and the warmth of her understanding encouraged me to confide my sexual dilemmas. She pushed back her soft hair where it had fallen over her eyes and, steadily keeping me in her gaze, began to place her thoughts before me.

'Our sexuality is a deep mystery. This is more than just a physical act. The whole of our being is involved in the unknowable depth of our sexuality. Sex is basic to us, yet infinitely more complex and spiritual than we can comprehend.' Her words, gentle yet profound, spoke to my soul. 'This is one reason why our sexuality is so open to misuse and why we are so wounded when it is violated.'

Here was a truth I needed to hear, a truth I could believe, shared with knowledge and love. I knew it instinctively. When we survivors were sexually assaulted, our very selves were debased. It is the area of our greatest vulnerability, for more than just our physical beings are violated: sexual abuse has injured us spiritually as well.

If I had just continued reading and accepting what I read in the Bible and never queried or admitted my opposition, maybe I would not have made this discovery about myself. Yet now it was the beginning of the easing of a terrible inner burden and confusion. Here was an answer, an explanation from God for my distress about being 'fearfully and wonderfully made'. It was abuse and maltreatment which had distorted my view of myself.

Seeing these concepts more clearly was helping me to acknowledge that my sexuality is part of the spiritual person who is me, not merely a physical act which had been grossly misused in my childhood.

My heart aches for those I meet who have also been degraded. Who can know the extent of that dire humiliation? Abuse and its after-affects have seeped into every facet of our beings, playing havoc with our normal reactions. Even though we were abused, we still respond naturally to sexual stimulus and have the usual physical awakenings. As children, these were often activated at the time of our molestation and this sense of physical pleasure has added to our guilt. This and worse indignities have produced devastating influences which have corrupted our normal sexual reactions.

For many survivors this has made our present sexuality fraught with confusion and disharmony, a vague dislike or a disturbing revulsion. I read that sexual feelings can be the most contradictory emotions we experience. This is one reason why unhealed sexual traumas carried into married relationships often produce a terrible inner conflict of wanting sex, but hating it at the same time.

Before I was to speak one night, my husband, trying to

look very serious yet unable to wipe the silly grin off his face, said, 'Don't forget to tell everyone that sex is also good, clean fun.' It's true we can achieve companionship and warmth, love and comfort and fun in sex. We can experience times of delight and ecstasy and, in an open, vulnerable way, share our very being with our chosen partner.

I have been blessed by marrying a considerate man who has shown me that to make love and become one with the right person can be a beautiful act of sharing. Still, Rob and I did have problems in our sexual relationships, for my father's violation and my mother's distorted views had produced reactions in me which sometimes, suddenly and without any obvious reason, made me opposed to any touching and loving, making me cold and distant. Then I would become very angry at this invasion of my person, would state that the whole act was utterly distasteful and repugnant to me and be quite adamant that it was totally wrong – though I did not understand why.

Even though Rob tried to explain over the years that it was God's special way for union between us, I still had problems. These could influence me during our lovemaking, for as well as becoming angry, my mind would fill with entirely unrelated thoughts which could completely turn me off.

Often we survivors are unable to respond as we would like to. Sometimes dreadful memories flash back into our minds, at other times fear or humiliation overtake us, and our bodies can react adversely entirely of their own volition. We can feel isolated even as we are sharing because of the secrecy and guilt forced upon us as children. This has probably set up a conditioning like habitual thinking which began at the time of our degradation and has continued to govern our sexual responses.

No matter how loving I felt or what I wanted physically, the use of my mind in this way was more powerful and, indeed, I have read since that the mind is a most important element in the act of sex. My mind would also control my desires and make it impossible for me to initiate any lovemaking, for within me were the repressed memories of that terrified child's passive submission and utter humiliation.

With the recollections of the defilement of my childhood another dilemma was added, for Rob – who had known my parents well – was at first unable to comprehend the truth of my past. Then, when he knew it was true – not wanting to add to my suffering – he began to withdraw from contact with me. Being me, with my usual habit of knocking myself, I thought I had become repulsive to him, while he feared any closeness would trigger within me a painful memory and revulsion because of the horrific experiences I was uncovering.

Realising we needed more help, we sought counselling and worked hard at resolving the misunderstanding between us. Slowly a delightful change is taking place in our love life. Now we feel freer to express our own personal desires and enjoy joking and being together.

A fact often not understood by many people is that the act of sex by itself for itself can rarely help us. Survivors are often misled into thinking and feeling that sex is the only thing they have of value to offer and that if they give themselves in this way it will ease their pain. This is not so, yet it can sometimes drive them to excesses in an effort to feel close to someone. Sex does not cure the aching aloneness and terrible fears which live within the molested person, nor sadly does it cure the desolation and unutterable damage inflicted on the spirit of a sexually molested victim.

Do not condemn those among us who are overly affected in their sexual behaviour by calling them loose-living. Think instead: *why* are they like this? Could we ever count the vast number of young people who are thrown into promiscuity and prostitution because they were plundered and violated as children?

The horror of one survivor, when only a little girl of three, was to be set up by her father for the use of his friends. How can we condemn those who have suffered in this way? How can they go on through life and be expected to act in a normal manner in their personal encounters?

Can we also try to understand that the reactions of some survivors may be to totally turn off from any sexual contact? Do not call survivors frigid. Is it any wonder that so many survivors are closed and cold or else too open, too free, when such gruesome things are done to little children? There seems to be an unnatural – almost hothouse – climate in which everyone is expected to perform sexually these days. I believe no-one should be pressured to conform to these expectations.

All this sends me back to the Bible and the Sermon on the Mount where God tells me how we should really treat one another. He is teaching me that I have been too hard, too rigid, not loving enough. I have been guilty, especially in the areas of others' sexual problems, of sometimes only pointing out the faults and not loving the person. How intolerant I have been over the years! I thank God for opening my mind and broadening my understanding of how it is for others and for forgiving my intolerance, without necessarily condoning their actions.

Such opening of my mind has enabled me to discover that, as survivors, our present reactions are largely the replay of the way we coped as children. An adult activity was forced upon us over which we had no control and to which our consent was never asked or given.

For this reason it is important that our supporters ask our consent in matters pertaining to us and do not just give advice or orders. This honours us as people of value, even though we have problems. It enables us to know we can begin to make life-changing choices. We can learn that we do not have to acquiesce in every situation now if we don't consider it to be right.

No longer do we have to be dominated by our past. No longer do we need to search for the unnatural yet perhaps only type of love and closeness some of us have experienced as children, no matter how warped it may have been. We can make our own choices now, because that inner person is ours to give or withhold. We are no longer forced, as we were as children, to expose our very soul for another's taking. We can choose not to allow or be involved in this any more. Beginning to understand these facts is enabling me to cope with much of the shame and hurt which was stored in my memory.

Yet there are still more hidden memories and fears in me, for when the Bible suggests – as it so often does – that I should draw near to God and have him draw near to me, I become afraid. I believe that for most people there is some apprehension, though often secret, at the thought of knowing God and especially being known more fully by him. But for survivors there is an added dimension of tension in drawing close to God, or other intimate relationships, because of a reaction in us caused by sexual abuse. It has set up a fear which frequently begins to constrict my breathing.

I know the breathing of many survivors is shallow, even difficult. Mine is. I was told that this was most probably caused by the awareness in the victim of the physiological changes that take place in the breathing of an abuser when he prepares to sexually molest a child. A change in breathing means something fearful and painful is very likely about to happen to the child. Further, the victims are powerless, unable to control the change in their own breathing in fearful response.

'I hear him breathing even now,' Mary had whispered fearfully to me one day.

The realisation that this problem with my breathing is still affecting me gives me more work to do with God. I know, because of past experiences of his activity in me, that God can help me again. So I'll need to ask him to amplify the difficulties associated with my breathing and then have him overrule these with me. I believe that God can show us how to change our responses, including our physical ones. He can help us with our choices and alter our broken values of ourselves. God can begin to teach us, as he did me from Psalm 139, that all his works are marvellous.

Though I had disagreed strongly with him on this topic, God is showing me that even my sexuality is his beautiful gift of love. I'm learning to appreciate that love, and respect and trust my choices. I do not have to remain subject to the fears, physical repercussions, secrecy and isolation which had previously held me in their debilitating grip.

It is not always recognised by those not involved that there is a terrible aloneness, an indescribable isolation, for a child being physically or emotionally abused and, especially, sexually assaulted. The sense that no-one knows but you and your attacker can leave a child desolate. So often it is impossible to tell your secret.

I have a friend who had never told a soul the facts of her father's molestation until she finally shared her gruesome story in her seventies. What a secret to keep smouldering inside all those years! What isolation and suffering this causes! I am slowly learning to ask God into the hidden horrors of my aloneness, particularly when it affects me now:

Isolation grips me, an utter aloneness.
Family, friends
skirt around the fringes
of my locked world.
Not able to penetrate the hard shell of
my isolation.

> I seem to be sharing, joining in,
>   smiling, laughing,
>   making small talk,
>   corny jokes.
> The polite interchanges not overcoming
>   my isolation.
>
> Within me another existence
>   unshareable,
>   unpresentable,
>   unacceptable,
> longs for someone to break through
>   my isolation.
>
> Yet is it such a bad thing, my aloneness?
>   God seeks me in it,
>   teaches me from it,
>   loves me through it.
> His presence can gradually overcome
>   my isolation.

Unless we face this isolation, accept that we are cut off and then have God work in it, it can turn within us to bitterness and hatred, and make it virtually impossible to want to forgive. Reading the Sermon on the Mount showed me what God wanted me to learn about the dangers of not forgiving. It burst through my cosy thinking and forced me to see the absolute necessity to forgive.

Who? My parents? The stark truth hit me that I did not want to forgive them. I know this whole concept of forgiving is very difficult for survivors. It seemed *impossible* for me to forgive my parents. God worked in me to enable me to do this and to tell this properly I have taken a chapter later so we can go into it in the detail it deserves.

There are some cases where forgiveness seems well nigh impossible. One of these tragic aspects, from which I have been mercifully spared, is pregnancy! There can be no doubt this adds a particularly heartbreaking dimension to the pain of survivors. So very many have borne a child, or even more than one baby, through the rape they suffered. For so many survivors, especially younger-age girls, often this did not stop at one pregnancy, for frequently they were subjected to two or even more.

Some girls have been assaulted, then put through the torment of terminated pregnancies; others have given birth to babies while fourteen years of age or even younger. They have had their babies taken from them, though sometimes they did not wish to give their consent. To add to their trauma, underage and unwed mothers are frequently the butt of society's callous and malicious treatment or· even indifference.

Although sexual abuse is perpetrated on girls and boys, the biological consequences can be much more devastating for a girl, for she is the one who can produce another life. I have young friends – their stories and pain tear at my heart – who have become pregnant through no fault of their own and have suffered alone, unable to expose who the father was out of dreadful fear of further reprisals. Children have been branded as bad girls and worse.

What mind-shattering stories so many tell of their desolation at the time and their lifelong remorse at what happened to them. All this was outside of their control – the blame was not theirs but another's – yet the shame was foisted onto these girls. Too many have spent their lives, often secretly, longing for the child they bore, never knowing what became of their baby.

No wonder there is anger and bitterness. No wonder forgiveness for the baby's father and agencies involved is fought against and almost impossible to grant.

One morning I woke early very depressed. A friend, now aged thirty, had told me the day before the terrible story of the sexual abuse she had suffered as a child. She had wept for the six pregnancies (all terminated) she had by her father and his friends and that, at fourteen, her first surviving baby, her darling son, was taken away. She longed for him. Her loss still caused inconsolable sorrow. There seemed no solutions.

I took my Bible, my heartache and my complaints to God out onto the patio. It was a dull, foggy day with damp, cloying, salty air sticking to everything. Not pleasant – just how I felt. When I read what Jeremiah said in the Bible, I cried with him to God: 'My eyes fail from weeping. I am in torment within, my heart is poured out on the ground because my people are destroyed, because children and infants faint in the streets of the city. . . What I see brings grief to my soul because of the women of my city.'

I began demanding to know of God, 'Do you feel this way, too, God, about child sexual abuse and its ongoing consequences? If so, what are you doing about it? Are you helping? How?'

Then I read: 'Because of the Lord's great love we are not consumed, for his compassions never fail. They are new every morning; great is your faithfulness.'

I demanded to know: 'God, does this heal the hurting? What does it do for the situation at the moment?' My whole being cried out, 'Oh Lord what can be done?'

Though my questions did not have immediate answers, at least it felt safe to ask them. At least I knew God heard. God knows. We do not need to be left alone, for I also read that God is distressed with our distress. He weeps with us! God understands. He has compassion for us, his broken children. His desire is for us to share our suffering with him, for if we cannot go to God. . . where can we go?

I am gradually seeing that I do not have to be afraid to go to God and draw closer to him because he treats me, as he has set out in the Sermon on the Mount, with fairness, forgiveness and faithfulness. Further, he wants me to treat others as well as myself in this way.

Those of you who are our supporters can treat us with these Sermon on the Mount standards. This will assist us to build new reference points and to grow from these. You can be with us as we face and work through our inner pain and the problems which emanate from our sexual abuse. You can believe what we tell you without condemning us and accept how hard we have struggled to survive. This gives us a sense of being honoured by you and encourages the process of valuing ourselves. It enables us to make the best choices we can. The encouragement of my supporters over the years has often given me the courage to go on.

Yet I know supporters find coping with us can cause them many heartaches. They often have misconceptions about how to act towards us, so here are some of these I've found to be decidedly unhelpful.

❑ Don't tell me it's all in the past, so why don't I ignore it: I've tried that; it doesn't work!

❑ Don't tell me it cannot hurt me now: I am often still hurting!

❑ Don't suggest it can't still be affecting me: too frequently, it still is!

❑ Don't tell me to get on with living: I'm a survivor; that's what I've been struggling my hardest to do for years.

Some supporters listen, think they know how I feel, then put me straight. Sometimes they give me a lecture, tell me to have more faith and to try harder. Or even thoughtlessly, ask me if I am really a Christian! They apply their solution, but I leave, reeling under another blow!

❑ Do not come at me to fix me as though you know how. Please encourage me to find my own answers and try to understand and respect these. This will show me I am not useless and worthless, but of value to you as well as to God.

❑ Do not try to stand between God and me, irrespective of your own beliefs. Allow me to come closer to God, for I believe that even with all my apprehension he alone can really meet my deepest needs.

It takes time for me to put into practice this step of reading the Bible in a new way and it requires quite an effort to write down all my thoughts on a passage, but the results are worth it. It stops me hiding from God and myself and shows me very succinctly how I really think and feel.

Better still, it begins to open up amazing things I believe God wants me to know: his wonder and sovereignty, his concern for me, how he planned me to be. All this enlarges my mind. Such Bible reading has become a vital step in my recovery.

18

My sixth step:
I grieve for me!

'MY INNER CHILD REACHED across the years to haunt me,' someone wrote. Ah, but not just to haunt me! To enhance my existence. The wonder is how often she bursts into my life with special fun, delicious joy and the surprises of spontaneity!

Would I swap all that to be rid of the pain and heartaches which ebb and flow through my days, from that same hurting little girl who also lives within the confines of my adulthood? No! Definitely not! Each part – the playful and prim, the cheeky and cheerful, the weepy, the hurt and broken – is an element of that unique person which was me, is me and will be me. For my child is alive throughout my whole life span.

Dare I ignore such a vital presence? I can, but to my great loss. For much of what I am now, or will become, has roots somewhere in what she has lived through, how she has coped and the adaptations she has made to everything my life has plunged her into. She is the storehouse for my earliest memories. That complex creature of pain, pleasure, passion and peace is me. Every facet of me is worth caring for, not least the child who was so badly hurt.

A survivor friend, having pondered this concept for many

days, finally said: 'That seems to be right somehow. The little girl who was abused is me. Caring for her, my hurting inner child, leads me on to care for the adult me. I can see that now. Maybe we are both worth caring for, after all!'

Can we understand this controversial idea of the presence of our child still alive within us, recognise its relevance to us now as adults and even go to the lengths required to grieve with and care for that young self?

Maybe the idea of an inner child is not part of the experience of many people, so I've tried to present another different angle from which to view the whole concept. I don't pretend this is an accurate psychological analysis: merely an attempt to explain a very tricky, but immensely important aspect of the lives of survivors.

Some people may not be aware of an inner child as such. For them, 'the hurting inner child' is a vivid metaphorical representation, a picture of aspects of their emotional life. My husband tells me he does not experience the presence of his inner child as an apparent separate entity apart from his adulthood. He assures me he sees himself as one adult who as a child had certain things happen to him. Now quite often he enjoys feeling *like* a little boy, being childish and having fun. He finds it great to still feel *like* a virile young man and is a bit frustrated when he feels *like* an old man. But for me there is a much clearer sense of division. It is as though I have an inner child who has suffered and still does, while at the same time I am an adult.

Many survivors and others may not recognise any dichotomy within themselves, but for those survivors who are aware of this division, I wonder if it has come because we've had to distance ourselves from our childhood trauma to enable us to cope? We became adult, in fact, before we even had a chance to be children.

The 'inner child who is hurting' is a way of describing the presence of some emotions which have been stored in their childhood state, because they were not nurtured but rather restricted by the trauma of abuse. From this we can begin to comprehend that we have our different basic reference points of defective nurture. This enables us to understand more clearly what is happening within us and the importance of learning to care for any fragmented parts of our inner selves.

How our inner child can still be affecting our lives is complex. I think about it in terms of a large circle representing the adult 'me', coping in varying degrees. Right in the centre of that outer circle is a smaller inner circle where I as a child still dwell and am hurting. As a child my responses to my world may have been entirely appropriate for an abused child – indeed, at times the way I acted could have been lifesaving.

But much of that childish way of responding and acting is not appropriate to transfer into adult life. Sometimes I act and respond in ways the child learned and never grew out of – a type of failure to grow and develop in a unified way in some areas. This is not exclusive to survivors: everyone has these problems, but for survivors they are more marked. That is why survivors' ordinary emotions have become the indicators of our abuse when they are exaggerated, extreme or too intense.

It's as though my inner child from within her circle is radiating messages to the adult 'me'. She may still be angry, ambivalent, terrified and deeply hurting – quite natural reactions from a child being abused. These feeling messages can grip me at odd moments entirely discordant with the adult situation, then they fade back into the innermost 'me', quiescent till the next time.

Through all this my inner child may be begging for, even demanding, my attention and approval, wanting my understanding longing for my love – still trying to obtain these from me fifty years later. As an adult I need to be seeking and working towards the two of us becoming more in tune, more congruent with each other. We need to come together, as a friend illustrated it, as the two sides of a zipper gradually become enmeshed with each other, so that the adult 'me' is no longer manipulated by the stored up horrors within the inner child, nor the inner child ignored by the adult.

It is as though at the time of my abuse I sealed my horrors in separate compartments. This was an unconscious device to stop my child-mind shattering. At last, I am unlocking these hidden places and releasing all that was stored there. Now, instead of being afraid, I'm finding this same process of compartmentalising can be used wisely and sensibly in adult situations to enable me to cope more efficiently.

Very likely the hurting child within us is still suffering from the trauma of abuse and is affecting our adult lives. God wants to bring support and comfort both to the grown adult and our little child. Rather than putting limits on God and allowing only a small space in me for his activities, I have chosen to follow the steps to open myself further to recovery. Over the years I've sensed that as my child was reaching out to me, I was reaching out to her. I asked God into that fear-filled place and he has entered my deepest pain, my hurting place, and is working to heal the ache in me.

Again a poem helped me pour out my feelings, expressing how it was for me:

> There is an ache in me beneath my smiling face.
> I ask God to enter and illuminate that hurting place.
> What do I find ?
> Wrapped in a shroud of anguish and terror,
>   deep within me,
> hiding in the corner of a dank, bare room,
>   cowers me, a small broken child. . .
>   Weeping.

Surely, child, you would have gone after so long,
    faded away or been expunged by my mind?
My very adulthood?
The maturity of my experience should have removed
you. 'Go away, wretched child!
Leave me in peace. Torment me not.'
All should by now be forgotten. . .
    Finished.

'If I relent, grieve with you child, assuage your an-
guish,
    then I, the adult, will be consumed by your sorrow.
    Broken too!
How will I cope if all and every hour I, too, am
caught
    in the horror of your ill-treatment?
Always experiencing, continually remembering
    that I was not wanted. . .
    Unloved.'

Can this be true, my parents, my God-given guardians
    failed to love and nurture me,
    abused me ?
I cannot face it.
    Fear to admit it. Dare not believe it.
    Will not accept it!
Knowing better, unmoved, the heartbroken child. . .
    Weeps on.

'I would rescue you, my child, but fear to try alone.'
Then Another, sadder, wiser than I, enters
where you are.
Pierced hands enfold with warmth, compassion, truth.
'Weep not, little one, I will release you.
Fearing adult, admit, believe, accept.
Take courage, we three can face it now. . .
Together.'

'I feel my child within me like that, too,' Bronwyn whispered, her voice soft with tears.

'Well, I don't!' Shirley was working at being extra tough. 'Of course, I feel hurt and damned angry. But I don't feel like I have a child inside who is me, too, like you're suggesting. That's *not* how it is for me!'

Our survivor's group was together again, discussing this step of caring for the hurting child within us.

'I don't know if many people, especially if they haven't been abused, feel like they have another person living in them, even if it is their own childhood selves,' Jane said, trying to understand the concept. 'But I do know what you mean and I think it's a very graphic picture. It helps to describe what I feel inside me very clearly.'

'I know my hurting child is still inside me and I want to help her. But how?' Mary was getting more courageous. 'This may sound a quaint question, but how do you get in touch with your inner child?'

'I think it's a very relevant question,' I answered. 'You can start by admitting that inside yourself things aren't how they should be, or how you'd like them to be, and you need help. We survivors often keep our suffering – our hurting inner child, I call it – hidden, even from ourselves. Or if you prefer, Shirley, we try to hide our emotional state from others and ourselves. So I'll tell you how I interacted with my hurt inner child – what I did about the suffering I felt.

'First, I asked God to amplify her, to help me bring her out and express her hurt. (Of course, you realise it's me as an adult who will experience all this.) Second, I acknowledged that my inner child's hurting presence was disrupting my adult life. I recognised that through helping her I was helping myself.'

'So how did you help her?' Mary asked hopefully

'That's my third point,' I answered. 'I began to search out ways I thought I might help her. I looked back over my childhood, but there was no true nurture to draw on. Then I thought about how I'd brought up my own children. That seemed a more hopeful avenue to follow. I loved them very much and, although my mothering was not always as good as I would have wished, I knew how I would have liked it to be.

'Sometimes I did OK, sometimes I made a hash of it. Yet I tried. If my children were hurt, I cared. If they were sad, I comforted them. If they told me something, invariably I believed them. If they wept, I, too, wept inside for them. If they lost something, we searched together. Their heartaches became mine. I longed to let them know how much I loved them, but often this didn't come over as I hoped. I wanted to give them the nurture they must have to grow emotionally. Best of all, I liked them.

'This brought home to me that, without consciously knowing it, maybe I didn't even like myself as a child or my inner child now. So I had to admit this and ask God to overrule my dislike of her and teach me to treat her differently.'

'Did you ever ill-treat your children?' Bronwyn asked.

'No, but I did take the whole child-rearing bit much too seriously,' I explained. 'I wish I'd cracked a few more jokes, laughed a lot more – that would have done wonders then. Looking back, I think my expectations were unreasonably high for my children and this might have discouraged them. I tried not to disapprove too strongly when they misbehaved, but I'd never learnt any other way to bring up kids. If you asked them, I know they'd relish telling you how I used to get mad at them and chase them with the fly swat.'

'Was your own upbringing a problem?' asked Mary.

'It kept getting in the way. But I didn't ever abuse them, nor did my sister, neither did our husbands – as some abused parents do. If I'd remembered my own childhood, I know I'd have done it differently – much less rigidly for one thing.

'I can see that it would really be worthwhile for young women and mothers to have God work in their lives,' said Jane. 'It would help if they faced their inner hurting selves, because that would enrich their children's lives and their own.'

'OK, so what did this have to do with caring for your inner hurting child?' Shirley chipped in.

'It occurred to me I could apply some of the same methods I'd used to bring up my own children to the situation of caring for my inner child. I figured it was certainly worth a try and I decided I'd definitely add many more principles I've learned since, that I wish I'd known back then.'

'I'm also suggesting that we make an attempt to believe and accept our own innocent child within. A special way to care for our hurting child is to *grieve for her and with her*. She was so badly hurt, she needs this. There is something very uniting in being able to feel for the pain and loss of another. To grieve together can bring about a reconciliation between us and our inner child.

'Recently I found something I had written when I began to grieve for the child in me: "I weep for you, that eighteen-month-old baby – so little, so afraid and hurting so much. I weep for you, that lovely thirteen-year-old with your laughing, vital face – clawed, battered and spat upon. I weep for you – *myself*." That grieving and weeping became an act of loving and reuniting.

'Another friend shared her experience with me: "I know

about the horrors of abuse. I've been there, too. Your body has mended, grown, become adult, but the inner core of your being – that little girl – was so wounded and damaged by your abuse, that only God can fix that. You need to ask him back into your inner hurting self and into your injured spirit. This probably is still your most painful place."

'Part of the pain is that we think we are just not worth looking after. This has been so ingrained in many survivors that we believe it. It may not be apparent to observers, but we have not learned well the skill of caring for ourselves, which tends to come more naturally to non-abused persons. They have not come from the same basic place as we have. Therefore we push ourselves, often beyond our endurance, or ill-use ourselves emotionally and physically.

"'I was a horrible useless kid," a survivor told me, her nose wrinkled in distaste. Her self-rejection as a child was obvious. Not so obvious, but equally true, was her rejection of herself as an adult. As a child she had never learned to approve of herself and now she was continuing the same way as an adult, treating herself as she had been treated as a child.

'How can you explain to a hurting child that they are still an acceptable person even though a parent, close relative, friend, or even a stranger has ill-treated and misused them? They view the situation with child-like logic. "Why shouldn't I be hurt? I wasn't worth looking after. So I am not worth anything much. I'm not worth caring for or loving." These are the childhood assumptions that are made.

'Does this type of assumption vanish as the adult grows older? Usually not. It may become hidden or overlaid with many external things such as studies, career, family, social activities, pleasure-seeking, success, even illness. But I believe it will continue to flow out from its inner circle each time an appropriate situation triggers it. That's why I choose to look at it, face it, then ask God to overrule its control over my life and enable me to grow on and through these assumptions about myself.

'At times our inner child is angry, bitter, resentful. Pain can express itself in these ways and, if we can come to the centre of our anger, we can begin to go beyond this and see the hurting child within lashing out, desperately fighting to survive through the horror of its betrayal. On the other hand, the inner child may show itself by over-submissiveness, fear and depression.

'When I was suffering from severe depression I sought medical help. "Hmm, change of life," said one expert. "Severe depression," said another. "Here, take these tablets – they will quieten you down," said yet another.

'No need! I was already down! What I wanted was a cause and a cure, not a stopgap. I wanted peace within me and peace with God.

'I knew I must come to grips with my inner child who was hurting so desperately. I came to see that I was condemning my own inner self. I needed forgiveness from myself, both for my adult self and my child self. Though my little child was not guilty, she was bearing that guilt. How often this happens with those abused as children!

'I began to listen and care for my inner, hurting child. What a difficult, frightening and utterly exhausting experience this can be. But though as an adult you will be heavily involved, you will be more able to cope and understand that the memories and emotions which are resurfacing were repressed when you had a child's perceptions. This is how it was all remembered from the child's perspective. We as adults can know that in time the pain will ease, a fact we did not know as a child. Yet, as with much recovery from child abuse, the process is slow, not easy, but very necessary. Take your courage in both hands and persevere.

'The very way we want our supporters to look after us is the same way we can learn to care for ourselves. It seems strange, but for years I knew I was in pain yet not aware that my inner child was still there, still active and very much in need of my care and attention. She was reaching out for me, her adult, to help her.

'I remember when my counsellor asked me: "Have you ever grieved for the hurting child in you?" I had to admit I hadn't even thought to. But now I know there is a definite part I must play; there are certain things I can and must do. I can learn to listen to, believe, accept, care for, grieve with, love and nurture that hurting little girl in me, for she was the one abused. I also have learnt that I must not lock this hurting child away again, rejected, denied and abandoned just like she was before. For me, too, it was important to ask God to manage the whole situation.

'One activity I really enjoyed as I began to encourage my inner child was to look at photos of myself as a young child. To my surprise I saw she was a nice little girl – I liked her.'

'That's special! What else did you do?' queried Bronwyn.

'I've heard of many ways that are now being used to help abused children face and share the awful things that are happening to them. As adults there are lots of ways we can express our inner feelings, too,' I said. 'We can make them concrete in some visible form. We know Bronwyn paints pictures, including angry ones. Jane's into pottery, getting rid of her feelings by bashing clay about.'

'You've all seen the beautiful shells I collect,' Mary said. 'I'm really proud of them. You'd be surprised how much I get off my chest when I polish them.'

'Did you know that I'm great at psychodrama? I can really express how I feel doing that,' Shirley rushed to tell us. 'And to save you blowing your own trumpet, Cathy, we all know you write.'

'Yep! But did I tell you that about a year ago I changed my format for once?' I replied.

'No, but you will,' came from Shirley.

I continued undeterred. 'My father was a sadist and, though he'd been dead for years, my terrified inner child was crying out to me for help because of the memories of his diabolical cruelty. I was so afraid, I felt immobilised in case my father played another of his ghastly tricks on me. He was so vicious I secretly called him "the fiend".

'Somehow I had to ease the demands from my inner child and face the terror and torment I was still trapped in because of Father's cruelty. Someone suggested I draw "the fiend". I'd tried writing to express my feelings in this area, but as I drew I began to see how I had envisaged my cruel tormentor. He was huge; I was tiny. He had two faces: one horrible and vicious, the other handsome and kind. He had dozens of arms all holding implements he had used to torment me. My arms were tied down tight. I was his captive.

'Suddenly I realised that was *then. . . not now*.

'That drawing was no work of art. Yet the relief it gave me was immense. I even raised a chuckle. Somehow, scrawling those lines and splashing them about with colours, released me from the pent-up fear I'd carried all my life, caused by the sadism which drove my father to intimidate me. I remember thinking that I'm an adult, too, not a little frightened child. I can take care of myself and my poor, inner Cathy. I don't have to be controlled by my father's cruelty any longer. The fiend has lost his power!'

'What a discovery!' Jane entered into it all with enthusiasm. 'Doing external things really does work to release our inner feelings.'

*   *   *

Now and then I see clearly another approach to my inner child, a way to get back to sharing on the child's level on her terms. I saw it one day when a friend and I went wandering around the rebuilt older part of my city. There were dozens of shops in quaint old buildings and old warehouses.

'Let's go into this one,' she suggested, pulling me into a puppet shop. 'I want to tell you how I use these in my work.' I was fascinated. She is an incest crisis centre counsellor, working with families and children in crisis now.

'Puppets,' she said, 'can help children to relax and open up. It seems quite natural for them to tell their stories to a puppet. Even the awful things which have happened to them can be shared with an agreeing puppet.'

She pointed out a strange-looking dragon puppet. 'It's extraordinary what a child's choice can tell you. I have a dragon puppet with two heads and the number of children who relate quite naturally to this two-headed being is uncanny. "That's like So and So," they tell me. "He or she has two faces, too!"

'Good and bad in adults seems to be understood easily by kids. Especially the hurt ones. Sometimes they get a puppet and have an animated conversation with my puppet. They often use this method to share their distress.'

My friend picked up a cuddly koala puppet, telling me more.

'A little boy came to see me. He was very quiet, didn't talk, wouldn't even look at me.' She slipped the koala over her hand. 'So I took out a puppet like this one and sat him up. The boy sat looking at it, while I wagged it before him for several minutes. Suddenly his "storm gates" opened and his terrible story of abuse flooded out, while his koala confidante nodded and understood.'

We both stood silently for a while, she remembering, me just holding back tears, imagining. Then she continued: 'Before he left he wanted to give "koala" a big hug, squeezing my hand tight inside. He'd found a friend he was prepared to trust.'

Our hurt, frightened, inner children need someone to trust. Someone who will not condemn. Someone who will listen, accept and believe their pain. Someone to weep with them and love them. That someone can be our adult selves. No matter how much love our supporters give us, wonderful as this is, it can never compensate for our own lack of personal, accepting love. Eventually we have to begin to love and accept ourselves and to believe that God loves us, too.

To love ourselves brings the nurture we did not receive as a child to our whole being. Slowly I'm learning it's not wrong to love my inner child, the inner me. That's what she needed most: to be loved – and she was not.

My inner child is beginning to blossom. The child who hid in fear is now emerging with all the many interesting facets of her personality.

Frequently I go to the beach; it has become a place of release, for I feel God's presence there. One day as I ran up a sand dune and over the rim – the wind catching my hair, blowing it back from my face, fresh and cool – there spread before me, mighty in its vastness, the sea. Free to ebb and flow. Free to pound the beach with crashing waves or gently caress it with a ripple.

Hope flowed through me, for I was no longer alone, I was no longer fighting against myself, my past, nor my God: I was breaking through. The joy of it soared in my soul, rising from the depths of my being and swelling upwards, bursting upon my mind with the truth. I, too, was becoming free for I had hope; no longer was I enmeshed in my own private hell.

Being given the courage to face my past – to change, to grow, to hand the control of my life over to a God I am learning to trust – is setting me free from the strangling control my parents had. Free to serve him and walk in his plan for my life. Who can know freedom like the one who has been in bondage? It seems the more terrible the chains, the more exhilarating the release.

The cheeky child in me, so long constrained, laughs aloud, shoes off, kicks up her heels and heads for the water. Down the hill, slipping, sliding, rolling over, sand flying. Wading into the foaming surf, skirt held high. Chasing the waves outwards as they retreat, then racing up the beach as fast as I can go, thrilled to outrun them as they advance. I hug myself in sheer delight, then dance across the dunes, high stepping, twirling, the music of Tchaikovsky's 'Nutcracker

Suite' lilting and vibrant, swirling and singing in my brain, my body barely able to contain its joyous elation.

A great love and gratitude well up within me, for now I have hope. God is with me. We can go on together.

19

My seventh step:
Release me!

'WELL, HERE'S A PARADOX!' Jane stated bluntly. This step is talking about us being released from the effects of our childhood abuse by becoming dependent on God. How can that be?'

'I want to be released for sure!' Shirley declared. 'But I don't want to depend on God. Why should we have to?'

'Because we have troubles, pain and problems in our lives and there doesn't seem to be anyone else who can help us in the same way as God can,' Mary said. The group was together again and Mary was getting more outspoken each time we met. 'I'd just love to put all my confusion and pain onto someone. It would help me. But I have to be honest and admit I still have doubts about God.'

'I'd like to depend on God to help me deal with my problems, too, but I'd still want to run my life my way,' Jane maintained.

'I think it sounds wonderful. Just to hand over the whole painful lot onto God or someone. And be released as well!' exclaimed Donna, who had joined the group.

'Does it all hang on our interpretation of what depending on God means?' Jane wondered. 'If so, what does it mean to depend and how can we do it?'

'Quick, Bronwyn,' Shirley rushed in, 'before Cathy gets underway. Tell us what you think.'

Bronwyn was quick. '*Depending* means for me relying on someone outside myself for support, maintenance, help, care – and lots more. When it comes to depending on God, I find it's having confidence and trust that he will supply all those things for me. And if I give him my hurts, memories, problems and every facet of my life, I then have to believe that these are in his hands and he is willing and capable of looking after me in them.'

'Are you saying,' Jane asked sceptically, 'that your problems will just vanish, like giving something away and never seeing it again?'

'Sounds like quite an idea,' Bronwyn answered, 'but no, that's not what I mean. I still have my problems, but I've done something particular with them. For me it's essential to know I've made a conscious act of giving them to God. When I've done that, I then have to believe he's working on them, too.'

'What's this *too* bit!' demanded Shirley. 'Either God has them or you have them.'

'Actually we both have them if I've given them to him,' Bronwyn continued. 'I have to keep living with them, but I'm no longer isolated, struggling away by myself. Now God is in them, too, so I can expect his support. When I give him my problems, it's as though I've made a move to trust him to look after me and do the best for me. I've made a choice to depend on him no matter what happens. I'm putting myself in a position to believe that whatever occurs is within God's purpose, irrespective of how things appear to be. I think if I can hand things over to God like this, it will be a great release for me.'

'The best option for me would be to be cured. That's what I want,' Donna murmured, 'and I'm not sure I can depend on God for that. But by the same token I'm not sure there's any other way either. So I'm stuck!'

'Me, too,' Mary admitted. 'I just want to be out of this pain. But I'm not sure I want to get into depending on God.'

'It appears to me,' Bronwyn said firmly, 'that what we want is something which doesn't work in real life, at least not quite like we're hoping it will. I'm not sure, but it sounds as though we want God to heal our hurts and fix our problems, while we go on our merry way without him. Like letting him pick up the bill.'

'That's just what I *do* want,' Shirley asserted.

We all grinned a bit sheepishly. Bronwyn and Shirley had hit the nail on the head. Having God wipe away our problems and release us from them would be wonderful.

Jane replied with a sigh, 'Underneath I guess we need to recognise that God doesn't just remove those things we don't like or want in our lives. It seems to be much more of a two-way street than that. Like us doing our part and God doing his.'

'Our part seems to be to learn to depend on God and I don't think that's easy for people who've been abused,' I said. 'It will mean a whole reversal of our thinking, a different way of viewing God and ourselves.

'If we knew that God would help us, look after us, release us from our problems and do the very best for us, how would that be for us?' I asked.

'Great!' came the chorus.

'Well, do we know that he will?' I asked. Another chorus: '*No!*'

'So why don't we know and believe that?'

'Because he didn't look after us when we were kids being abused,' was one answer. Another was, 'We don't know how to trust. You've said it often enough. Our trust was violated as children.'

'I pray and hand my problems over to God and I don't get the answers I want, nor the ones I hope for or expect – or sometimes even deserve,' Mary said, sadly.

'That's right!' Jane responded. 'Me, too. I keep giving

God my problems and asking for his help and I don't seem to be getting any relief.'

'Do we think God wants to look after us then?' I asked again.

'Hell, I don't know.' Even Shirley was on a down slide.

'Look!' Bronwyn spoke up, 'I think we're coming at this whole thing from the wrong angle. I've a feeling that what we're saying is this: we had a bad time as children and were hurt so much and feel so betrayed, we think that proves God doesn't care about us, isn't likely to want to look after us and that, if we give him our problems, he *won't* look after us. That's habitual thinking, isn't it? What we need is another authority outside our own biased one. We need some concrete evidence that God will look after us whether we feel it or not.'

'What sort of evidence?' Jane asked.

'The stories and teachings of the Bible, for one thing.' Bronwyn's enthusiasm was infectious. 'We've talked about how it's opening up our minds to what God wants to teach us. As well as that, we can follow the story of many people's lives and God's determination to bring good out of evil. Like in Cathy's life. I've known her for years and I can see a big change in her life, particularly since she began doing the steps.'

'But you still have problems and trouble coping, don't you, Cathy?' Donna queried.

'Yes, lots of times I do, but depending on God isn't a formula or an insurance policy to take away our problems. At least not for me. I think I have to rely on God in spite of what happens to me and how I feel.'

I was searching for words to explain what I meant. 'For me, depending on God is being willing to go out on a limb and act as though God will really take care of me, no matter how I feel or what the circumstances are. It's acknowledging my position with God: knowing my place as his child and accepting his place as my God, and finally being willing to let him look after me his way, not mine!'

Shirley was getting very cranky. 'Do you all know what Cathy is saying that "depending" means? We put aside ourselves. We do what those lousy words like overrule, submit our wills and obey actually suggest: we have to bend to depend. I'm not into that!'

'Yes, that's what I mean,' I said. 'I have to be willing to put aside what I want and make a definite choice to depend on God. Then, no matter how much I disagree or can't see what's happening behind the scenes of my life, I have to keep making that same choice again and again. I need to change my habits and my will so that I begin to depend on God. The odd thing is that I'll ask him to help me do this very thing, because I can't achieve it without him.'

'But what if God doesn't give you what you think you should have?' Mary was perplexed. 'What if the pain still stays?'

'I think that's where the steps would come in,' was Bronwyn's generous comment. 'Following them helps, because they are all stages leading us to depend on God more. You could tell him that you believe he isn't answering and giving you what you believe is right. Then you could ask him to overrule that and manage your life for you.'

Muffled groans from Shirley.

Bronwyn smiled, ignored her and went on: 'There's no doubt in my mind that God will ease your pain, but he expects you to participate by sharing it with him and trusting him whether you feel as though you're able to trust him or not. Even if you don't understand why things happen as they do, you can still begin to learn to trust and believe that he really will do what's best for you.'

'But I don't think I *do* believe that God will really do what's best for me,' Mary said hesitantly.

'I think that's the crux of the whole problem,' Jane summed up. 'Life with God seems a sort of balancing act. Will he do the best for me, won't he, or what will he do?'

'I'd find it very helpful and a whole lot easier if I knew *what* God was going to do – what his solutions are for my problems,' announced Shirley.

'But what kind of solutions will they be?' said Mary, sounding suspicious.

'God's solutions to our problems may not be what I'd have chosen, often they won't be easy ones, and at times they can be quite unusual,' I replied. 'He doesn't always solve my problems. Yet surprisingly, his answers enable me to cope even if they leave me in the same old circumstances. God's solutions to my problems haven't given me health or wealth. But they have given me something less easily defined, less visible, yet more valuable: a workable, worthwhile relationship with God.

'I may not always have obvious physical security, but I'm learning slowly that with God I have something my soul has longed for even more. If I will accept it, God wants to give me spiritual security. He is showing me that he loves me. The amazing thing for me is that God hears and he works. God produces his own answers. Sometimes God's solutions seem simple, but I frequently discover they have deep implications in my life.'

'But do they help you? Do they meet your needs?' Mary asked.

'As a general rule, I can look back and see that through all the traumas in my life, God was with me meeting my needs: he *did* look after me,' I mused. 'Not always as I would have planned – often far from it! His care has not been conventional and yet I believe the resolutions he has brought about are far better than the ones I would have chosen for myself, though I don't always recognise that at the time.

'I think God is trying to teach me to depend on him more, but so often I'm in a rut, hanging onto old hurts, strangling myself with them. I'll tell you what I mean with something that happened recently.

'The phone rang fairly late one night. It was bad news.

It hit me very hard. The old pain grabbed me and tore at my heart again. I had thought it was over; I thought I'd given it to God. Yet here it was again, rising up to smash me down.

'I cried out: "God, why? What are you doing? Why aren't you looking after me and my family? Why are you letting this awful thing happen to us?"

'Immediately I turned on God and blamed him. I hadn't meant to. It just burst out. After a while, the weeping and anger subsided. Then came a frightening discovery. I had accused God of not looking after me, just as I had done when I was a little girl being abused by my parents. The same old reason surfaced: it must be my fault. . . I'm no good.

'I felt overwhelmed at my reaction. After all these years of learning to trust God, now when I needed to I didn't. "Well, that's who I am," I decided. "That's me; I don't always trust." True as that statement may be, I could no longer hide in it. I needed to face this new, but so old sense of having been deserted, rejected by God again.

'Some problems I've depended on God to deal with have been resolved the first time I ask and that's a great relief. But there are some hurts which seem to take a long time to work out. I seem to be dealing with this habit of blaming God, yet for years feeling it was really my fault. Here was my hurt child again. I no longer needed to respond this way.

'Several weeks before, when I was feeling unhappy, I asked God to *amplify* my fear that he could not be trusted, because I wasn't worth looking after. I asked that he *overrule* this fear, then put the whole thing out of my mind. Sometimes when we ask God to manage our lives, our situation appears to get worse. Here I was in a deeper trial, a harder battle and desperately hurting again! This seemed to me to be a strange answer from God.

'I've noticed before that this is how God operates sometimes. It's as though he is testing me by asking, "Are you serious? Do you really want to depend on me right now?"

'Here it was again, clear and concise. I couldn't miss it. I must make up my mind. What was my attitude to be? Was I going to scream endlessly at God that he had failed me? Was I going to wallow in self-pity? Then the thought hit me forcibly: Was I going to stay as I was forever? Was I going to feed my anger against God? Was I planning to remain the same and let this come between me and God and control me, run me, fuel me?

'It brought me back to reality. I was relying on something inside myself, something I had kept within me for years. I was not relying on God. I was living on what I call "a fuel of my existence". I was being driven by an old attitude I had been clinging to for years.

'What to do? Was I going to depend on God, take this further step and co-operate with him in dealing with this devastating conviction that he was failing me? Would I give it to God, or hang on to it, live off it, be motivated by it?

'Here was a scary moment. The feeling that God would fail me had been haunting me for years. Did I have the courage to give this to God – maybe lose it forever? Did I really want to?

'I don't always want to change. Sometimes I even seem to have internal resistance to healing and growth. I'm used to my behavioural patterns. I've been acting and reacting certain ways for over fifty years and I'm not sure how I will be motivated without my fears and habitual ways of functioning. A decision had to be made. I knew that I couldn't even do that correctly by myself. I needed God for that, too. So I asked him to overrule this old consuming attitude and to work it out his way. Another barrier had been lifted between God and me.

'I still ached. The pain, the hurt were still there from the bad news, but now it was as though a path had been cleared. I could take this step and depend on God without recriminations and not be dragged back into my usual mind set. God was breaking the control of my past. I had laid my pain before him and wept with him. I was learning to depend on God more, though he wasn't always taking away my problems, but rather he was sharing them, doing his own thing with them. I realised, too, that depending on God meant accepting his decisions for my life and his authority.'

'Told you so!' was Shirley's comment.

'I know the steps have done wonders for you, Cathy, but it did help to find out about your past, too, didn't it?' Donna asked. 'I think if I find out more about my past, that will be the thing which will really heal me and I won't need to do any steps or worry about God any more. Will I?'

'It didn't work that way for me,' I explained. 'When the incidents of my parents' cruelty first began to erupt from my memory, I thought that finding out about my past would bring about my recovery simply by exposing it. But it began to dawn on me that just knowing those things did not alleviate my suffering, nor heal me. I discovered that reliving, though relieving, is not necessarily *releasing*. In fact, seeing the pictures of my past again tormented me even more.

'Nevertheless, I do think it helps to relive some of the incidents, because representative pictures can reawaken the emotions experienced at the time of the abuse. It is the fear, rejection, horror and other emotions which return with the memories that need attention. We also need help with any adaptions we have made to enable us to cope with the past. These emotions and adaptions had caused me many problems and I was now trying to come to grips with them.

'Our son as a teenager was taking his responsibility of bringing up Mum very seriously. When I asked him if he'd mend my transistor radio, he said, "Have you checked the batteries?" I told him I hadn't and I wanted his help. "Look, Mum," he replied, viewing me with mock severity, "I'm trying to teach you to stand on your own two feet."

'There's a paradox here because I believe that's what God wants – for us to learn to stand on our own two feet and become more like he planned for us to be, but at the same time to understand that the more we grow and are released to increased personal freedom, the greater the necessity for us to depend on God.'

The group and I talked about the best way for our supporters to be involved in our lives, too. 'We need those who care for us to give us their perspective. It's essential for them to be firm with us and not let us wallow in self-pity. What a thin line of love those who support us must walk! They need to be kind and strong, yet understand that survivors are conditioned to expect rejection, unpredictable behaviour – even cruelty. Expecting the worst, we can read these hostile attitudes into situations and imagine they are present where they don't exist.'

Supporters, please try to bear with us when we make what appear to be irrational statements. We may be trying to tell you, if you listen carefully, where and how we are hurting and in which areas we are particularly in need of your understanding. Most of all, each of us can blossom with your patience and love, for which you deserve our heartfelt thanks. And, believe me, there is great value in being able to joke and laugh with each other in the midst of facing our pain and growing together.

When I speak in public, there is usually a barrage of questions afterwards. Actually I enjoy this part immensely, though once I was set back on my heels by a lady who rose majestically from her chair and witheringly addressed me, loudly and precisely, from the middle of the hall. 'I feel most indignant and demand to know how you can make jokes about this very distressing and painful topic. "Adults who have been abused as children" is no laughing matter.'

I agreed. I don't think it's funny either, but when you are speaking to people who are blowing their noses, sobbing and in deep distress, I find it eases the tension enormously to inject a few jokes. I try to keep a light touch, because encouraging adults suffering from the effects of childhood abuse through the ups and downs of recovery is a fairly heavy topic. One night a man even asked me very seriously, 'Is it essential to have a sense of humour to recover?'

My reply was obvious. 'No – but it sure helps!'

So does patience. It's one of those attributes which seems to have been eroded by abuse. I'm not just making an excuse here for any lack of patience in me, though it does help me to see why I'm deficient in this area. Children who have been deprived of love or natural care are often terrified to have to wait for anything of any nature, because they feel that if they don't get it straightaway, it may never be theirs, may never happen. Yet one of the solutions I know God often gives as an answer to my problems is to wait:

Wait ! Wait ! I cannot wait, I want it now.
Must have it now. It may not happen if I wait.
I need it immediately!
Sooner for preference, because I can't wait.

That's what's so hard, so unproductive,
hanging about, just to wait!
I wait without patience, or expectation,
I wait, just to fill in the time.

There's a pressure in me, an impatience;
there's a demand to get going – do it now.
'Wait for the Lord,' I'm told. 'Take heart!'
'Help me to wait, Lord. But fix it now!

'Can't wait' takes over my thinking. Controls it.
Demands my attention – deflects it.
Consumes my interest – dominates it.
Sidetracks my praying – ruins it.

Lord, overrule my impatience.
Teach me to depend on you,
learn to rely on your timing
and rest myself in your wisdom.

The comments of an overseas visitor caused me to stop and evaluate what I really did want in the matter of dependence on God. A self-possessed, capable and charming middle-aged woman, she confided to me, 'I often have to meet with modern young women who are competent, quick-thinking, capable, self-possessed and attractive. People like that make me feel so inferior.'

'Me, too,' I admitted.

'I wish I was like that,' she added rather wistfully.

I almost agreed again. But then I realised that if I was as great as they appear to be, if I had no problems, I just wouldn't need to depend on God for anything. I'd be on top myself. There's no doubt having that status appeals to me very much. But deep down inside me I know I don't really want that.

What I do want is the release, the freedom that comes from depending on God.

20
My eighth step:
I choose to forgive

ABUSE LEAVES SCARS to disfigure or adorn our tomorrows.

Scars are never attractive. Yet some are shown by their proud owners on every possible occasion as though to say, 'These are my scars. I'm proud of them. Look what I've been through; see how well I've recovered!' Or maybe: 'Poor me. Look how I've suffered. I'd like some sympathy.'

Internal scars cannot be displayed. Even the ones we have struggled with and overcome can't be clearly defined to show to admiring friends. Because emotional scars are not visible. Telling others about the cause of our scars means putting the whole activity into words and this is a tricky, complicated procedure. Yet we, too, want to display how well we are recovering.

Survivors will always have scars: not necessarily the visible ones, though some of us will even have those to bear witness to the horrors of abuse. Our emotional and spiritual scars become part of us and what we do with them goes on into eternity. But they no longer need to impair our lives, even if at times they still hurt us, just as any scar can if it is scratched or bumped. Our suffering can have purpose, though I don't understand how; it doesn't have to be wasted.

God did not shrink from suffering. He used Christ's

suffering for a great purpose. It was a poignant revelation to me that after Christ's resurrection, he still had the physical scars in his hands. For many people, these very scars have become a symbol of God's love towards them.

Suffering doesn't have to be destructive: it can be constructive, the start of a whole rebuilding process within us, working to strengthen the structure of our growth and development. The emotional and spiritual scars which once stultified our growth towards maturity can, if we choose, enrich our lives and the lives of others.

But these facts can seldom, if ever, be appreciated when the trauma is happening. Suffering is never easy, never pleasant and, if it has been lifelong and secret, there have been many painful years to undermine us. I remember telling God in a fury of despair that he had made a mistake when he made me because mine was a whole life wasted.

In her book *Walking on Water*, Madeleine L'Engle writes: 'The unending paradox is that we do learn through pain. . . Pain is not always creative; received wrongly, it can lead to alcoholism and madness and suicide. . . Nevertheless without it we do not grow.'

The choice is ours whether our suffering becomes of value or remains forever worthless, whether we let our pain touch our creativity and set it free to blossom, or permit our basic potential to wither because we fail to allow our creative abilities to escape from the clutches of our suffering. I know the lasting scars from vicious misuse can be redirected to beautify the lives of survivors; I'm thankful and relieved that God can and does do this for us, but again the choice to give him that option is ours.

'Choices! Most of my kids don't even know they have choices!' my crisis counsellor friend exclaimed.

Many of us can't see our choices or, if we can, do we know how to act on them quickly and rightly? Frequently we act a certain way because our previous choices lead us subtly and insidiously on, as though we are trapped on an endless spiral staircase, winding ever downwards, forced by our former decisions into the vicious cycle of our past suffering and ingrained habits.

These automatic reactions can be broken and retrained. Here I want to jump in and suggest we ask God to overrule them and help us give every aspect of our choices to him. Reshaping my automatic reactions has been one of the invaluable ways the steps have worked in my life. They have smashed through the rigidity of my decision-making processes and altered many of my previously held views on God and myself.

Yet if you have been following the steps suggested, I wouldn't blame you for thinking they were leading you on to make choices which could destroy you as a person or turn you into an obedient automaton acting against what you wanted for yourself. But this is not so. The steps are a series of choices which, if followed, can set you free to make more worthwhile, life-enhancing decisions.

I believe one of my most life-changing choices is to want to forgive those who abused me. Forgiveness is extraordinarily hard to do. But more than that, I find it an indefinable concept. My responsibility is to choose to forgive. In and through this God is moving, bringing about a change in the situation, yet I am still totally involved. I've never been able to fathom the inner workings of the wonderful changes forgiveness produces in relationships. Fortunately, my understanding of the workings of forgiveness are not necessary to make it effective.

To forgive is to pardon with compassion, to free a person from the consequences of their guilt or to pass over a blameworthy action without censure or punishment. Yet we are equally free to go on becoming more embittered by our past – filled with hatred against our abuser, our world, our God and, sadly, ourselves.

I am not suggesting that because we forgive, this condones or blots out the diabolical actions of abusers. These will always be criminal acts of the most base type. Forgiveness is a generous move by one hurt person to another whom they believe has harmed them. Most especially, it is God's move to each one of us.

A letter I received brought out this whole area of forgiving our abuser with beautiful simplicity:

'Yesterday at work,' wrote a social-worker survivor-friend, 'I had to counsel a man who had cancer. When I was speaking to him, he started to tell me how ashamed he was of his life. He had been married several times and had abused his wives and children. He was so full of guilt and shame, but knew there was nothing he could do about it. He was most upset because of what he had done. But he also said that he had had a happy life – he'd had fun. It was they who suffered. Now it was his turn to suffer.

'I started to realise that the only hope for this man was God's forgiveness. I knew God cared for him and could remove his guilt, but this man was not interested in God. I felt like crying – he was rejecting his only hope.

'After I left him, I became angry – angry that he rejected God and angry for what he had done to his wives and children. I started to hate him and yet I couldn't forget his pain. Then I acknowledged that he was human and he needed forgiveness, just like me.

'I thought back over my life and thought of the pain and guilt those who had abused me would feel because of me and then I started to hurt for them. It was the first time in my life that I've ever seen the hurt and shame that they would feel. I've never thought about it from their side. I began to feel like I could forgive them. I had no need to make it harder for them – they were going through enough. If God could forgive them, then I could.'

This perceptive young woman had captured something of the immense healing and restorative power of forgiveness. At a cost to herself, she had made a choice which is turning her life round and setting it in a new direction.

What price forgiveness? From my friend's letter, it may appear as though she had found forgiving a fairly simple process, but this is not so. Forgiveness is hard to do – for God and for ourselves. For God it was immensely costly – the death of an only Son. Many people don't conceive of the cost to God, yet are fearful of the cost to themselves, particularly emotionally. I think that's one reason they prefer not to become involved and choose not to forgive.

Another is that something in us insists that not to forgive is just: that revenge is just; that to foster our hate and bitterness is just; that we have a right to these attitudes and offenders are not worth forgiving. Or that it will somehow demean us to forgive, appearing to excuse their crime in doing so.

I understand survivors' reluctance to make a further sacrifice and forgive. I can almost hear some survivors claiming: 'Why should we forgive? We were the ones wronged. We are the ones who have suffered our whole lives because we were abused.' I understand that reaction so well:

Revenge is mine; I've earned it,
through all the years of suffering
from the evil abuse in my childhood.
But it is not sweet.
    To contemplate it gives me no pleasure.
    It eats at my very being.
    Anger and hatred fill my heart with pain,
    my eyes with coldness.
        I have cause for them all,
        even self-destroying bitterness.
        They are justified, right and proper.
        I was most terribly wronged.

Yet where is the joy ?
Where the longed-for release?
Why am I still enslaved
by the pain from my childhood?
There is no freedom in hating.
It does not affect the offender.
It eats up the one who is hating,
and heaps more sorrow on sorrow.

In what, then, lies my release?
Anger, revenge have failed
to ease my endless aching
and stop it stifling my soul.
The answer, 'You need to forgive them',
seems futile, weak, ineffective.
The apparent foolishness of forgiveness
led to Christ's death on a cross.
How can the act of forgiving
defuse my anger and suffering?
Overcome my ceaseless strivings,
give me an inner peace?
I don't know how forgiving
washes away the dirt of hating,
leaving me clean and peaceful,
freed from desire for revenge.
A miracle lies in forgiving.
What wonder it works in my soul!
Such pain it removes, then by giving,
God fills my being with love.

Paradoxically, in choosing to forgive, we benefit immeasurably. No matter how poorly we do it, God steps in and responds. He also works the miracle of tearing down barriers and restoring broken relationships between us and others.

An amazing fact about forgiving is that we are no longer helpless victims. We take the initiative. Then when we do ask God to help us forgive our abusers, it breaks their control which (though I don't understand how) seems to still dominate our lives, as the abusers did when we were children – even though our abusers may now be dead.

Two sisters in their thirties told me that they had asked God to help them forgive their father as he lay dying in hospital. 'When we were little girls,' they said, 'after our mother died, he abused us. Every night, until we left home fifteen years later, we barricaded our bedroom door against our father. And every night he came and noisily banged on the door, kicked it and yelled, or furtively turned the knob, attempting to break in. We lived in fear and terror in case he succeeded and then abused us as he had when we were younger. Now, after all those years of terror, we wanted to forgive him.

'Our dad didn't die then. He lived long enough for us all to be able to discuss together and work through the fear, anger and hatred which had festered in each one of us all those years. This eased a burden which we had all been carrying. We are the ones who received when we made a choice to forgive.'

I remember when it was suggested some years ago that I forgive my parents, this pulled me up with a jolt and opened up the subject from a whole new perspective. I had not wanted to forgive them. I remember giving vent to my strong feelings and shouting, 'Why should I forgive them? They don't deserve it! Anyway, they are dead. What difference can it make now?' I was to find out that I could be changed!

I knew it was right to forgive and I felt the need to forgive them. I was aware of a bitterness in me when I refused to forgive and this was affecting my interactions with my husband and children. For me to forgive was essential for all my relationships. Nothing can alter the circumstances of my childhood; only my attitudes can be changed – and one attitude that needed changing was my lack of forgiveness.

One way to forgive that works for me is to ask God to let his forgiveness flow through me out to others. I ask him to forgive in this way because I know how impossible it is for me to even want to forgive at times. This is especially true of my parents, because memories and anger, pain and disgust about them catch me still at unexpected moments. I guess I will never forgive them completely, but I can become involved with God in forgiving them again each time I need to.

But we survivors need to be forgiven, too. 'Hold it! Hold it right there!' Shirley's voice stridently cut in. 'We weren't the ones who did the abusing.'

'I'm not suggesting we need forgiving because we were responsible for our abuse,' I answered, quite surprised.

'Why then?' queried Mary.

Before I could reply, Jane laughed and said; 'I know all you girls and not one, not one of us, has lived our lives without ever hurting others or failing and generally making a mess of our own living and relating.'

'We've all hurt others and need God's forgiveness for that . . . at least!' Bronwyn acknowledged, then continued. 'As I see it, unless we understand and accept our own guilt, we don't think we need forgiveness. Yet whether we believe it or not, we do.'

'I think that's right,' I added. 'The more we allow ourselves to accept our own guilt, the more we appreciate God's pardon and the substitutionary death of Christ for us. I used to think forgiving was for the sake of others. I now know it isn't only for others; it's for me, too. When I forgive, it sets me free from bitterness, anger and hatred. Of course, these feelings can and do rise again. Forgiveness works again, too!'

'One thing that has surprised me is that to forgive, I don't have to believe the other person was right,' Bronwyn said pensively. 'I don't have to believe they didn't mean what they did, nor that they couldn't help themselves. I don't have to make excuses for them. I can see them as wicked, cruel, power-hungry or however I recall them. What I can do, and what is best for me to do, is to ask God to forgive them and help me forgive them *irrespective* of what they may have done.

'I'm finding out that to forgive, I don't even have to like the other person. Yet the amazing thing is my feelings can undergo an extraordinary change when I do forgive and I may grow to like them – or even love them.'

'All you've just said interests me very much,' Mary stated, 'because I would like to have a reconciliation with the person who abused me, but I'm not sure if I should.'

'Don't do it!' Jane interjected very strongly. 'I know of a survivor who wrote to her abuser seeking to be reunited, but was cruelly rejected again, causing her more heartache.'

'Well,' Bronwyn added, 'I feel it's important to know that forgiving is our responsibility; accepting forgiveness belongs to the offenders and we can't control their actions. They can choose not to accept us or our forgiveness, and deny that there is any question of it.'

'. . .because they might think that accepting forgiveness indicates an admission of their guilt,' Shirley concluded.

'It seems to me that often we, also, refuse to receive or forgive to our own indescribable loss,' I replied. 'I believe that God is always offering us his pardon. He never stops, because forgiveness is basic and fundamental to God and our need for it is equally as basic and fundamental.'

'I think that's right,' Bronwyn agreed, 'but frequently we don't receive it, because we don't ask, we refuse to accept it, or we ignore God's offer. So we block ourselves off from the release of being forgiven. This can start us again on our cycle of hating and hurting each other and failing to take the healing, preventative measures of forgiving.'

'If it's really worth having like you say,' Donna said shyly, 'then I think I want it. What do I have to do?'

Bronwyn said gently, 'You just ask, Donna. . . that's all you have to do. It's always there waiting for us. Ask God for his forgiveness: he'll begin to do the rest.'

We sat quietly, very moved. After a while I said, 'I've wanted so much to tell you something wonderful that happened to me recently. Through all of my growing and changing, I felt something was missing. A special spark. I wondered what it was. Now I've found out. It was the experience of *feeling* God's love. I know God has always loved me, but I don't always experience the joy of that; I don't always feel he loves me. On some occasions when I choose to forgive, this most precious experience of my life takes place. I receive an extraordinary gift from God. I feel his love.'

I then recounted to them something of this heartstopping, delightful discovery. It feels to me like I've found an amazing secret, which has been sitting there all my life just waiting for me to unlock and grasp it. Not a secret at all!

It was always open, always there for the taking. But I didn't know how to take it fully. It's simple really. Forgiveness is not just a stern command forced upon us. It is a key to open another door of responding to God and to each other. When I forgive, God doesn't just remove the wrong, the hate, the meanness and leave an empty space: God fills it; he gives me his love. But this experience is not something we can always expect to happen. While God always loves us, it is up to him whether he gives us the sense of his love. God's activities cannot be programmed to work as we would want, or to our timetable.

God's priceless gift of love fills me with wonder and gratitude. I, who did not think I deserved to receive anything, actually am given love by God, a gift which is of inestimable value to an abused person. My excitement at receiving God's love in such a definite way may seem exaggerated to some people, but it is clear to me and very precious. I understand it in the context of my abused childhood.

My expectations of being loved were shattered when I was a tiny baby and I had continued to believe that I was unlovable all my life. I now know, through my family and others, it's not true. Now I find God has showered his love on me. I will never be able to express adequately the joy I feel in that. I'm sure it's special for everyone to know that God loves them freely. But for me, a survivor, it is wonderful. Now I find I can love God in return.

I've often wondered what love really is. The Bible has a mighty description of love in the first book of Corinthians, chapter 13 which is worth reading. God loves us like that, though humanly it is impossible to achieve. I found a description of love in M. Scott Peck's book, *The Road Less Travelled*, which seemed to fit for me and is easier to put into practice: 'Love is to extend oneself for the purpose of nurturing one's own and another's spiritual growth.'

At the core of this love is forgiveness. This forgiving love offers freedom from the physical debilitation of holding grudges, disliking others, coping with guilt, fearing in our relationships. When we are able to ask for forgiveness for ourselves and others, we can be willing to be vulnerable and open, not afraid when others hurt us emotionally.

Of course, domestic violence and physical attacks come into another category and we do need outside professional help in these situations, but *the aftermath of all problems can be forgiven*. I can ask God to forgive in every situation and then I can receive the love which comes as part of forgiving. It makes me want to cease counting the cost of forgiving and to throw myself open to its influence. I feel such awe and gratitude that God would do all this and so enable me to have these gifts of love from him.

As I have written the steps, I've asked myself these

questions: What are they achieving? Am I recovering? Are the steps working for me? What's in them for other survivors?

I have looked at myself. . . and have seen what? That I am more together, more at ease, even more trusting, less self-hating. I see a woman still in the thick of life, often thoroughly enjoying it. I am participating in life's pains and pleasures, not removed from them, not unmoved by the ordinary happenings of living, whether they hurt or not.

I see me, knowing and accepting the fact that I have suffered, yet facing life; not fleeing from that suffering, but learning to use it creatively; watching my recovery taking place; admitting that I have come a long way these last eight years, a very long way. Nevertheless I am still me: still given to sadness, though it no longer consumes me; at times angry, but now it's more clearly directed and controlled; sometimes suddenly assailed by feelings of worthlessness, though these happen less and are not as acute.

There are times when I'm still overtaken by grief for the hurting inner 'me'.

I'd always had a secret hope that to recover would mean somehow becoming close to perfect. Now I know this won't happen. Someone said: 'After you have worked through your repressions, your past, and acknowledged your sins and failures, you don't end up perfect; you just end up as yourself.' When I heard this, I was struck with disappointment. I realised I wouldn't be an entirely different type of person after all. No. . . I'd still be me!

But there is an element of delight in this, for God created me to be the very person he had in mind from the first. Yet his transformation is not restoring me as I might have been without the abuse; rather he is adding to my life, rounding it out with all I have learned from my childhood experiences.

A friend said sadly: 'Just below the surface of my life is a layer of tears. That's where I've kept my pain for so long.' Then she enthusiastically added, 'But you have given me a tool, something to enter my internal pain and know it can be dealt with by God.'

These eight steps are that tool and I use them constantly to participate with God as he changes the inner 'me'. What a relief to be able to tell God how I think and feel about him and myself. It never ceases to amaze me how absolutely effective God's answers are when I ask him to overrule my self-centredness and other aspects of my life. By applying the steps, I can have him show me myself here in the present and amplify my past so that he can work his will in it all.

The way my Bible reading has come alive with God speaking to me through the words, and the release of being able to give him my hurts and depend on his solutions, leaves me with a quiet sense of gratitude to him. I'm thriving on the fun bubbling up from my inner child and watching us blossom together. My life is opening to the joy of forgiving and being forgiven. The wonderful discovery that I am loved by God and others permeates my life, infusing the darkest, most damaged recesses of my being. I am emerging from my journey through pain. I sense the wonder of recovery in me and I know it will continue.

There's a gentle, growing acceptance and valuing of the person who is 'me'. Alongside this, my suffering has shown me my great need of God – of someone I can rely on as I could never rely on my parents, others or myself. Most especially, I am learning to know God better and, as I do, to trust him more.

www.ingramcontent.com/pod-product-compliance
Lightning Source LLC
Chambersburg PA
CBHW050113280326
41933CB00010B/1079